WORKBOOK PRESS LLC
187 E Warm Springs Rd,
Suite B285, Las Vegas, NV 89119, USA

| | |
|---|---|
| Website: | https://workbookpress.com/ |
| Hotline: | 1-888-818-4856 |
| Email: | admin@workbookpress.com |

Ordering Information:

Quantity Sales: Special discounts are available on quantity purchases by corporations, associations, and others. For details, contact the publisher at the address above.

Library of Congress Control Number:

| | | |
|---|---|---|
| ISBN-13: | 978-1-963718-67-6 | (Paperback Version) |
| | 978-1-963718-68-3 | (Digital Version) |

REV. DATE: 01/18/2024

# TWISTED TRUTH

by

## Sharron Lee

# CHAPTER 1

From an early age, Sandy Johnson dreamed about living on a tropical island surrounded by the beautiful sound of waves lapping the hot sand. While a tropical breeze cooled the effects of the hot sun beating down on her. She was so determined to live her dream she got a job at eleven years old stocking shelves in a mom-and-pop corner store. She began saving every penny she could to make her dream come true.

She talked to her aunt who was a self-made millionaire about how she should invest her money. Her aunt also gave her books to read on investing. She carefully investigated every savings step she took to maximize her investments.

By the time Sandy was in her mid-twenties, she was a good-looking young lady who turned men's heads when she walked pass them. She had a particularly good paying job overseeing several nutrition businesses in several nearby towns. She also worked with an inventory company and as a bartender in her spare time. Sandy had become a workaholic who was obsessed with saving money. She had over a million dollars with her stocks, bonds, and three condos that she rented out. She was well off and awfully close to making her dream come true.

Then she met Thomas Stevenson who wanted to be a stockbroker in the Cayman Islands. Sandy was thrilled that she found someone who wanted the same thing that she wanted. He was still going to university, but she was willing to wait another two years to fulfill her dream. They planned to get married the next summer. Then they would move to the Cayman Islands after he graduated. Sandy continued working hard and saving money while Thomas was away at school. In her spare time, she planned their wedding in Costa Rica.

One year later, Thomas and Sandy were married on the resort's beautiful beach surrounded by twenty-one of their friends and family members that had made the trip to Costa Rica. The wedding vows were said with the sound of the ocean waves caressing the hot sand, a cool breeze coming off the water, and the sun beaming down on them.

Sandy's long white wedding dress fluttered with the wind. Thomas stood in his grey suit and baby blue shirt. His outfit complimented his light blue eyes that did not leave Sandy's face as they both smiled and said their wedding vows. Afterwards everyone had photos taken, before they went to the bar for drinks while their table was readied for the feast that was being prepared for them. It was one of the happiest days in Sandy's life.

When they returned home, Sandy started the process of getting the needed paperwork to get them moved to the Cayman Islands.

There was a long list of things to do to get them there. She got so involved with the making of her dream come true that she forgot to register her marriage with the Canadian government. She still was working the three jobs besides overseeing the construction company, she had hired to finish the basement in one of the condos, so she could rent it out for more money. She figured the income from the rentals would help them until they got established in the Caymans. George Becker was the construction foreman on this job. Right from the beginning George flirted with her but Sandy rebuked his advances.

Sandy was ecstatic when the paperwork for their move to the Caymans arrived. She danced around the living room singing, "I'm moving to the Caymans. I'm moving to the Caymans."

Sandy called Thomas. "Honey, we got the paperwork to go to the Cayman Islands. I will have us packed up and ready to move by the time you are done school in a week."

"I am going to be here a few days longer because they are having a job fair. It may help me to get a job offer in the Caymans," Thomas told her.

"Ok, I will have everything ready. Love you, bye now."

"Bye, I will call you after the job fair," Thomas said.

Eight days later, Thomas was at the job fair when he called her.

He told her, "My graduation ceremony is going to be in two weeks. Are you going to be able to get off work and be here with me for the graduation ceremony?"

"No problem I can be there. I gave my employers notice when I got the package from the Cayman government," said Sandy. "In a week, I will be unemployed and free to go to the Caymans.'"

"Oh...ok," Thomas stammered as he wondered how he was going to tell her about the decision he had made.

"Have you got a job offer yet,"

"No...eh...not yet but it still is early in the day," Thomas said. "I will be home on Wednesday. Then we must make plans to go out and celebrate and make plans to come back for the graduation ceremony. See you then," Thomas said as he wondered how he was going to tell her about what he had done.

"See you Wednesday," said Sandy as she wondered if Thomas would get a job today.

When Thomas got home, Sandy was dressed up and ready to go out to celebrate. She was like a kid on Christmas Day.

He had emailed her and told her he had good news. She was expecting him to tell her that he had a job in the Cayman.

"What is this good news?" Sandy said as he walked in the door.

He took her hand and lead her to the couch.

"It is great news. I was offered a fantastic job and I took it,"

Thomas said with a big smile on his face.

"I knew it. When do you have to be in the Caymans to start work," asked Sandy?

"No, the job is here in town," Thomas answered.

"What! What about living in the tropics? We have all our paperwork done ready to go. I quite my jobs. Our belongings are packed up ready to go. We made all those plans. I even gave you most of my money to transfer to an account in the Caymans," Sandy said as tears welled up in her eyes. She felt like she had been stabbed in her heart with a knife.

"I thought about it and decided this was the best way. I will get experience here and then I can put out feelers for jobs there. It is better than moving there and hoping that I can find a job with no experience," Thomas tried to explain to her.

"Why didn't you tell me about this? I feel like you did this without caring about what I wanted and need. You went behind my back to get your way," Sandy said as tears ran down her face. "Why didn't you stop me from quitting my jobs if you wanted to stay here? Why didn't you talk to me first before you accepted the job? Do you even care about what I want?" she said as she grabbed a tissue from the box on the side table and blew her nose. She felt so hurt and betrayed. Her dream was shattered after all the years she had worked to make it come true. Could she ever forgive Thomas for hurting her so badly?

"With this job you will not have to work ever again. You can stay home, and I can take care of you. We can have a family as soon as I get my student loans paid off," Thomas said as he tried to convince her that this was a great opportunity for them. "In fact, it looks better if you are not working to my clients. When they learn that you are not working. It tells them that I am successful at what I do," Thomas said trying to convince her that his idea was the best.

"I am used to working and being out among people. "What am I going to do sitting at home?"

"We will be entertaining a lot and going out to parties that will give you something to do. You can go out to lunch with your friends.

We can have children as soon as my student loans are paid. There is a lot of things you can do."

As the days turned into weeks, a rift grew between them.

Thomas worked in the office all day and then went out in the evenings to talk to potential investors. While Sandy, a workaholic, was left sitting at home with nothing to do. She did not give up trying to persuade him to move. When that did not work, she pleaded with him to have a baby to fill her empty hours. He refused making her feel even more hurt by him. When she could not stand it any longer, she went out and got a job as a bartender again. This infuriated Thomas. They began arguing as Thomas tried to keep Sandy isolated at home. Sandy needed to be out among people, and she would not give up her job. This caused more friction in the marriage and Sandy felt hurt and unloved by Thomas.

Thomas asked her to plan a large birthday party for Thomas's friend. She worked for days decorating the house and working out the dinner menu. When Thomas did not even come home. This angered Sandy. All their friends asked where he was, and she did not know what to tell them. She sat drinking and watching the other couples having fun. While she sat worrying about Thomas. Where could he be?"

She was surprised when George Becker showed up. He had come to give her an invoice on the drywall work he had finished.

George started flirting with her when he learned that Thomas was not there. Every time her glass was empty, he refilled it. By eleven o'clock, Sandy was so drunk she could hardly stand up. George helped her up the stairs to her bedroom. She did not remember any of this.

At two in the morning, Thomas walked in and found them in bed asleep. He started screaming at her that she had betrayed her wedding vows. He was furious.

She pleaded with him to quiet down because her head was splitting, and she felt like she was going to throw up. She never felt this sick before. She tried to tell him; she did not remember what happened. She was so drunk.

George jumped out of the bed and stood between them. "Don't you dare hit her."

"What did you do to my wife? shouted Thomas.

"That is between Sandy and me," George said with a smirk on his face.

"I don't remember anything that happened," Sandy muttered as she ran to the bathroom and spent the next twenty minutes puking.

Thomas grabbed his suitcase out of the closet and started throwing his clothes into it. All the while screaming at Sandy saying he wanted a divorce. He stormed out.

Thomas showed up at Sandy's parents' house at six in the morning pounding on their door. When Sandy's mother, Lynda opened it, he burst through the door and blurted out that Sandy had betrayed him and was fooling around on him. He told them that he wanted a divorce as soon as possible.

Sandy's parents were stunned. They knew Sandy loved Thomas. What had happened? Thomas complained that Sandy had got a bartending job and she turned into a party animal. He never mentioned that he had broken Sandy's heart by trying to force her into staying home and not working. He also complained that all Sandy wanted was to have a baby. He never mentioned that she wanted a baby to fill her lonely hours sitting at home. While he wanted to pay off the student loans first. He blamed her for the entire breakup. He then told them that he had found her in bed with another man. He never mentioned that she was drunker than she had ever been before.

After Thomas left, Lynda called Sandy, but she refused to tell her mother anything that happened. She had such a bad hangover she did not want to talk to anyone least of all her mother.

Her parents worried about her. She had given up her good jobs. How was she going to pay for the condo that they had moved into after they got married? They also did not know that she had money.

When Thomas went to get a divorce, he was told that in the eyes of the Canadian government they were not married. Sandy had been so involved with getting the paperwork done to move to the Caymans that she forgot to register her marriage license. This infuriated him. To get back at her, he did not tell her the password to her money in the Cayman Islands. Instead, he kept the money for himself.

He also took over the condo's mortgages. Sandy wanted to

sue him for fifty percent of their assets, but her lawyer told her she could not because they were not legally married.

Sandy was shattered in more ways than one. She went from a financially secure woman with a dream of living in the islands to a poor broken lady who lost the love of her life and her dream. What made it worse was the love of her life had been the one who hurt her the most. He would not listen to her explanation of what happened. She took all the blame for the breakup and never told her parents the truth until years later that Thomas had taking all her money.

In the months after Sandy's breakup with Thomas, she shut down if they mentioned anything about finances or what was going on with the divorce.

Sandy's parents did not meet the cause of Sandy's marriage breakup until Christmas Day. George was a muscular, handsome, construction foreman who spent the entire visit trying to impress her family. Sandy was trying hard to be happy and bubbly, but Lynda wondered what Sandy really felt about this man. She did not seem happy. Had she settled on him because she was punishing herself for what she had done to her marriage? Her mother just watched and wondered. Sandy made sure that she avoided being alone in a room with her mother who she knew would ask her questions she did not want to answer. They did not stay long after they ate and opened their presents. They said that they had to stop at his brother's houses with presents for his nephews and nieces.

Several months later Sandy called Lynda at work.

"Hi, Mom, just calling to tell you that I am quitting my job, I am moving, and I am expecting a baby."

Lynda was so shocked at what Sandy had said she blurted out, "How are you going to care for a baby without a job."

Sandy immediately blew up at her mother because she did not make a fuss about her being pregnant. "I am pregnant. You are going to be a grandmother. You should be happy for me. Not worried how I will keep the baby. I am not stupid. George will take care of me," she started yelling at Lynda while her mother tried to get a word in.

Eventually she slammed the phone down hurting her mother's ear. Lynda did not know what to think since Sandy had not mentioned George in months, so she had thought they had broken up. Lynda did not call her back because she was at work and had already made a scene which the boss had heard. Lynda called her that night when she got home but there was no answer.

The next night, Sandy called her mother and again started yelling at her saying that Lynda had caused her to have a miscarriage. She told her mother that she never wanted to talk to her again and slammed the phone down.

Lynda did not know what to do. Sandy had not told her where she was moving to. No one in the family could remember George's last name. They finally realized that they were never told his last name at Christmas. When Lynda tried calling Sandy back, she got the message that the phone was no longer in service. Sandy's parents did not know how to contact her. Computers and Facebook had not crept into their lives yet. With Sandy living so far away they did not even know any of her friends that they could call. Lynda and Bob could not do anything but wait for Sandy to call them.

Twelve months later, Sandy called her mother to tell her that she was a grandmother to a three-month old baby girl named Patricia. She invited her parents over to see their grandchild. Sandy told her parents that they were living in the basement of Pat's home. Pat was George's father who was dying of cancer. George had moved in to help his stepmother take care for his father.

A week later Sandy's parents pulled into the large yard which had a line of man toys. There was a large fishing boat, a travel trailer, two motorcycles, two trailers, and two trucks.

Bob, Lynda's husband, asked George who owned all these items. George told them that he owned most of them and his father the rest of them. That made Bob less worried about Sandy's financial situation. It meant that George really did make good money.

They spent the afternoon admiring Patricia, the newest addition to the family and catching up on lost time. After they had dinner out, Sandy's parents left to tackle the three-and-a-half-hour drive back home.

Sandy and George were only in that house for a few more months when Pat died, and his stepmother decided to put the house up for sale. Lynda at the time wondered why George had not tried to buy the house from his stepmother until Sandy told her that George had a new job, and it was in another town.

Sandy was so excited on the phone when she told her parents about the rent-to-own cottage that they had found. She could not wait to move into it. George was going to fix it up just the way she wanted it. When Lynda asked them why they did not buy the house outright.

That is when Sandy admitted to her parents that they had just gone bankrupt eight months before this because George had not paid his bills and his income taxes. Sandy said that as soon as the bankruptcy cleared, they hoped to have a good deposit saved so they could buy the house from the newly widowed lady who owned it. Lynda had been told that George made fifty-two thousand dollars a year. Why couldn't he pay his bills Lynda wondered?

They settled into the cottage and began going room by room painting and fixing it up the way Sandy wanted it. George worked every night on it and Sandy called every week to tell her mother everything they had done to the place. She also let Patricia talk to her on the phone which delighted Lynda.

Three months later, Sandy called, "We have a surprise for you guys."

"What kind of surprise?" asked Bob who had answered the phone.

"George and I are going to be married. The house is all fixed up, so we decided that we are going to have a small wedding in our back yard with the money his father left him. It will be on Saturday, August 30th at 4 p.m. I am calling everyone and verbally asking them to come because the wedding is only four weeks away. Will you be there?"

"Of course, your mom and I will be there," said Bob.

"I am so glad. I will see you then. I will talk to you later. I am trying to get everyone called today," Sandy said and hung up the phone.

The day of the wedding, Sandy was so busy her parents hardly got to speak to her. She was busy taking care of Patricia, greeting the guests, showing the caterer were to set up and getting the music system and lighting system plugged into the house's hydro system.

While George talked with his family members and other guests.

She finally disappeared into the house to change into her wedding gown. Bob was called to go into the house in preparation of walking her down the aisle. While Lynda and Bob's mother sat in the front row and saved a seat for Bob after he gave Sandy away. The wedding was beautiful as they said their vows under a trellis with flowers growing over it with the setting sun behind it. Sandy held Patricia who was in a cute little white dress with feather wings and a halo of feathers on her head. They looked like they were extremely happy.

After they were married, everyone moved their chairs to tables set up on a platform that George had built under the tent, he had set up. We ate and danced the night away. Sandy and George moved around from table to table until they got to Sandy's family who were all sitting together.

Lynda told Sandy, "It was a beautiful wedding, but you hadn't told us that your divorce from Thomas had come through."

"It didn't. I forgot to register the marriage in Canada so in the eyes of the law here I was never married to Thomas."

"But you did marry Thomas, which makes you a bigamist," questioned Bob.

"Only if I go to Costa Rica and I doubt that I will ever visit there again," Sandy said sadly as George came back over to her and told her that they were ready to serve dinner. The rest of the night was filled with dancing, laughter and talking with the other family members and holding the baby until her bedtime.

Lynda and Bob did not get to see much of them because of their work schedule and the long drive to get there. Sandy would call weekly usually with good news but three months later she called to tell them that they would be moving again. The cottage's sewage system backed up after the ground froze. They were told by the plumber that they needed a brand-new sewage system installed. The roots of the trees in the back yard had destroyed the tile bed.

When they talked to the owner of the cottage about the problem, she told them that she did not have money to fix it. George began to dig up the system but before he got too far, they received a call from the bank. The bank informed them that the owner had not paid the mortgage in three months. The bank was taking the house back. They wondered if George and Sandy wanted to take over the mortgage.

Their bankruptcy would not allow them to do that, Sandy was faced with the job of moving again but this time she was a few months pregnant.

# CHAPTER 2

After moving three more times and having three children in four years, Sandy was ecstatic when one of George's relatives agreed to buy them a double wide trailer in a beautiful, treed trailer park. All she wanted was a place to call home and never have to move again. She wanted a stable home to raise her children in.

Sandy was a true stay-at-home mom because the trailer park was several miles from town. She rarely got the three children up, dressed, and fed to leave the house at 7:30 a.m. in the morning to drive George to work. Then she had to wake them up from naps quite often when it was time to go to pick him up from work. When she did, it usually meant that she had three cranky children on her hands for the rest of the day.

Sandy's parents tried to help her by selling her their old van for one dollar when they bought a new vehicle. With her youngest child a few months old and the oldest child starting pre-kindergarten, they thought that she needed a vehicle to go to the doctors, the school or even just to pick up things she needed for her family.

Within one month, George had taken over the van saying it was a better vehicle for him since he could carry lumber and other things that he needed on job sites in it. He convinced Sandy that if they sold his old car, they could pay off some of their debts. Soon Sandy was back to being stranded at the trailer park with three children. She did not know at the time that George had an ulterior motive. If she had the car, she would be able to do the banking and the paying of the bills. George could not let her do that if he wanted to keep his secret.

Sandy always checked to see how much was in her account before she went grocery shopping. She had started doing this after she discovered that George was taken more money out of the bank and not telling her. She got caught two times at the grocery store having her debit card rejected because there was not enough money in the account. When she questioned George, he told her he was buying things like cigarettes, gas, and lunches even though she packed him a lunch every day for work. Creditors started to call saying that their bill had not been paid but George had told her he had paid it.

She began to wonder if he had a girlfriend on the side. He did take off quite often under the guise of going to see a family member or he had an odd job to do for someone, yet she never saw extra money from the odd jobs.

She had had three children in four years, so her figure was not like it had been when they started dating. She also realized that she fell into bed each night exhausted from chasing three children all day.

She decided that she had to lose weight if she was going to keep her husband interested in her. She got an over-the-counter weight loss product to help her lose weight faster. She also started exercising to gain her figure back. George did not seem to notice the difference and George's spending did not change.

In fact, things got worse. If George were sent to pay a hydro bill of one hundred dollars, he would pay them eighty dollars instead.

When Sandy questioned him on why he had not paid the bill in full. He would come up with an excuse. She started asking for receipts for every penny he spent. This made him angry. He would give an excuse like the receipt blew out the window of the van as he was driving, or it fell into a mud puddle when he got out of the van. Their bills were slowly growing larger and larger. They were never paid in full or on time. They were getting calls all the time threatening to shut the utilities or phone off. They would get one paid and another would start calling. Their credit rating was in the basement.

George was making more money than Sandy's parents who both worked. Her parents were not struggling financially. George tried to blame Sandy for spending to much on the children. To prove him wrong, Sandy bought the children's clothes and toys at garage sales or thrift shops. Their furniture and household items were also bought this way. Sandy tried everything to save while George was spending more and more money without any explanation. What was he doing with it? She even went to the food bank when they did not have any money for food.

When George's relative called Sandy two months later saying that she had not received the mortgage payment for the trailer that month. Sandy panicked. She did not know what to tell his relative. George told her that he had paid it the week before. Sandy had even called the bank to make sure that amount of money had left their account. When George came home that night, he swore that he had paid his relative. She wanted to believe her husband but the nagging thought that she had no receipt to prove that he had paid his relative haunted her. Where would the money have gone? George said he would go see his relative and get the matter settled. He left and came back a few hours later saying that everything was okay.

One month later, George's relative called Sandy again. This time she was angry and proceeded to tell Sandy that she planned to evict them at the end of that month for not paying the mortgage. Sandy was stunned. George had told her that he had made the payment to his relative. Sandy's dream of raising her children in their own home was shattered again by a man who said he loved her.

When George got home, he was met at the door by an incredibly angry wife who was demanding that he tell her the truth of where he was spending the money, he was taking from their bank account.

"Did you pay your relative the mortgage payment last week?" "Of course, I did," George said.

"Then why is she evicting us at the end of the month? You told me that you had talked to her and that if we paid an extra one hundred dollars a month for the payment, we supposedly missed she would let us keep the place."

"I didn't give her the extra one hundred dollars. I needed it to buy a tool for the fancy cabinets I am making at work."

"From what she said you have not paid her one cent on the mortgage this month or last month." "Yes, I did."

"George, we are losing our home. The place you begged her to buy for you," Sandy said with tears streaming down her face. "What is going on with you? Do you have a girlfriend that you are spending your money on?"

"No," George said with a stunned look on his face.

"I can't take anymore lies," Sandy said firmly.

"I did pay it. She is mistaken."

"Where is the receipt," Sandy demanded.

"I err...I err...don't have one," George stuttered.

"I can't take anymore. If you cannot stop her from evicting us by paying the mortgage, the children and I are leaving you?"

"I did pay him," George stated firmly.

"Your relative is a smart person with lots of money. She would know if you paid her or not because she would have it marked it in her record book so do not lie to me. Did you lose your job again? Is that what is going on?"

"No, I just needed it."

"Needed for what. I have had enough if you don't tell me now, the children and I are leaving you and we will not take you back into our lives until you start telling the truth."

"I just needed it. OK." George shouted at her and then walked out of the trailer slamming the door behind him.

George did not come home that night and Sandy did not know what to do. She was stranded there.

The next day a phone call brought Sandy more bad news. The hydro company was going to shut the hydro off the next day if they were not pay their bill in full. Sandy panicked. Sandy had to keep her children warm. It was October. Every day the weather was getting colder.

She went out to the shed and found a roll of heavy-duty plastic and her husband's staple gun. She came into the trailer and proceeded to start stapling the edge of the plastic to the trailer's ceiling. She stapled it into a large rectangular shape making a tent shape in the living room. She overlapped the opening so that it would keep the heat in.

She then went to her neighbour and asked if she could plug into their hydro to keep her children warm until they could pay their bill.

She gave the neighbour her grocery money to pay for the hydro in advance. She then got the one-hundred-foot extension cord from the shed and strung the line out from the neighbours through her kitchen window and into her makeshift tent. She then got plywood and cut the size of the window with a notch in the corner out to allow just enough room for the cord to go through. She fitted it into the window and sealed it with silicone to make it airtight. After that, she found her small space heater and her electric fry pan. She now would be able to keep her children warm and fed. She dragged the mattress and blankets off her bed and put it in the tent area. She waited for the children to wake from their naps. As they woke, she dressed them up in warm clothes and brought them and some of their toys out to the tent.

She cooked all the meat in the freezer making things like chili, stews, and burgers. She put them in containers and stored them in the freezer to keep them as cold as she could. These were things she could warm in the fry pan for meals. She also checked her can goods for things like canned spaghetti, soups, and other quick meals that the children liked.

She told the children that they were pretending to camp like the story that she had read them a week before. She then waited for George to come home. She was going to get to the bottom of this because she had to protect her children.

When George came in the door, he stopped dead. "What is going on here?" he asked when he saw the tent with the children in it.

"We are prepared for when the hydro shuts off tomorrow,"

Sandy said angrily. "I want answers now, George. Enough is enough, I must protect these children from what you are doing behind my back. I need answers now or we leave."

"Don't leave. I love you and the children," George said. "I don't want to lose you."

"Then start talking," Sandy demanded.

"OK, OK. Remember I told you about the bad fall off the ladder at work I had before I met you."

"Yes…" Sandy said.

"When I fell, I didn't tell the supervisor because I had just started working for that company a few days before. I did not want to lose my job and it was my fault that I fell. I did not connect my safety harness up like I should have. I did not even go to the doctor because I thought that I had just bruised myself and I just needed time to heal. To combat the pain, I started taking over-the-counter pain killers, but I took so many to take the pain away that they eventually they did not work anymore.

I then went to the doctor to get pain killers at first. Eventually he refused to give me them because he suspected that I was addicted to them. I am addicted to them.

I took my father's pain killers. The doctor just filled the prescription whenever Dad needed a refill. When he died, I was forced to start buying them on the street. I should have told you, but I feared losing you," George said with tears in his eyes.

Sandy felt like she had been kicked in the stomach by a mule. She realized that she had never known George when he was not high on something. She had lived a sheltered life. She knew nothing about living with an addict. Especially, one who was a master at lying. She was not even sure that she wanted to. She already had her hands full with three children. George was already spending more that they could afford on drugs and that cost would only increase as he needed more and more drugs to kill his pain. How would she protect and support the children if she stayed with him? How would she support them if she left him?

"I owe a drug dealer a lot of money and he told me that if I didn't pay him, he was going to break my leg." George whined, "I wouldn't be able to work and earn money to pay all our bills."

"You won't have to worry about supporting us. I am leaving

you until you go to rehab and get off the drugs forever," Sandy said. "How are you going to survive with the children?"

"I will go on Social Assistance until you get your act together." "Where will you live?"

"Well not here since you made that impossible. I am going to either find an apartment for us or go into the Women's Shelter. Is that why we had to move so often? You used our rent money to buy drugs,"

"Well…eh."

"What did you do?"

"Our wedding cost us so much, I couldn't pay those bills and the rent. I made excuses to the owner for not paying the rent and she believed me."

"You mean you caused that nice old lady to lose her cottage and supplement income. How about the last house? I know that I brought the rent money and put it in the hiding spot she told me to use. Were you the one who stole it?"

"Yes," George quietly said.

"She accused me of lying to her when I told her that I had paid the rent. That is when she told me that we had to get out as soon as possible. How did you know where the money was hidden? I never told anyone where she told me to put the money." asked Sandy.

"I…eh took Patricia on a ride into the woods behind the two houses. I parked the four-wheeler behind her house and took Patricia into the garage with me. I asked her to tell me where she saw you put the money. She ran right over to the old trunk and pointed."

"You used your little daughter to steal money for your habit.

That is disgusting. I feel like a fool. I defended us when she accused us."

"I needed the money," whined George.

"We will be out of your way soon and then you can spend all your money on your drugs."

"No, I don't want to lose you guys."

"Then go into rehab and get cleaned up." Sandy said firmly. "We will not be a family again until you get off drugs completely. I will not put the children and myself through constantly moving because you owe money to your drug dealer. That is not good for the children.

I am not spending my time worrying how I will pay the next bill because drugs are more important to you than your family."

The next day the hydro was shut off and a few hours later a lady from CAS showed up at Sandy's door. The lady was prepared to take the children away from Sandy until she saw what lengths Sandy had gone to feed and keep her children warm. The CAS lady realized that the children are safe with their mother. She would do anything to keep her children safe. The lady helped Sandy set up her move to the shelter if she had not found a place to live in before she had to get out of the trailer. She also got emergency money set up, so Sandy could pay first and last month's rent if she found a place to live.

Sandy tried to find an apartment to go to that was big enough and cheap enough for her and the children. She used the neighbour's phone to make calls to the landlords. She paid them for the use of the phone, but she was running out of money. Her problem was that she had to wait for George to get home before she could go look at the places. By then the landlords had already rented them out, or they were to much money for her, or they were not big enough for her family.

Every night, she had to listen to George begging her to stay with him and every night she had to defend her decision to leave him until he stopped using drugs. Three days before they were to get out of the trailer. George did not come home. The phone was not working so he could not call her. Had he given up and abandoned his family? Or was he off somewhere using?"

Her neighbours let her use their phone to arrange for a mover to come in on the last day at the trailer to move their belongings into a storage unit. She had arranged to go into the shelter once she got their belongings moved. Still George had not come home. How was she even going to get to the shelter? She did not have the money for a taxi to take her. All the money she had left she needed for the movers. As the day ticked away, Sandy became more and more upset and worried.

While Sandy was fighting to get her children to a safe warm place, Sandy's mother, Lynda was worrying about her. Sandy usually called her every week. When she did not Lynda tried to call her, but the phone was not working. What was going on Lynda wondered? As the days went by and her calls did not go through Lynda became more worried that something was wrong. Finally, Lynda and Bob, decided that they were going to make the three-hour trip to visit Sandy and her family.

# CHAPTER 3

I t was a beautiful day, but it was cold out. Lynda and Bob had no idea what they were heading into. When they arrived at the trailer, they did not see any movement and there were no lights. When they got to the door there was no sound. This was strange since Sandy had children shows on the television all day because she believed it helped the children to learn.

Bob knocked. The door opened, and Sandy stood there in her coat. She began to cry and fell into her father's arms. She then hugged her mother and lead them into her plastic tent. Lynda went over to the three children who were all bundled up in sweaters and warm pants with blankets wrapped around them. They felt cold to her touch, and they had runny noses and were coughing.

"What is going on here?" Bob questioned.

"George didn't pay the bills and we are being evicted by his relative tomorrow. We have not had heat other then this heater for the last three weeks. The kids all have colds, and I am almost out of medicine for them. Tomorrow, I am to go into a Women's Shelter with the children until I can find a place to move into."

"What happened did he lose his job, so he couldn't pay the bills? asked Lynda.

"No, he used the money to pay off his drug dealer. He is addicted to pain killers," Sandy said sadly. "He didn't come home the last three nights. I have no idea where he is."

"What are you doing about your belongings?" Bob asked.

"I have some movers coming later today to move everything into a storage unit. I thought you were them. They should be here in the next hour."

"Well, we will get your belongings stored and then you and the children are going to a hotel tonight and get a warm hot bath and hot food into all of you. We will get medicine on the way," Bob said.

Sandy and Bob worked at getting the last things packed ready to be moved to storage while Lynda fed the baby a bottle. She then got food ready for the other two children.

When the movers arrived, Bob took over making sure everything that was to be stored was taken. Sandy and Bob installed the car seats into Bob's van, while the movers filled their truck with Sandy's belongings. They followed the movers to the storage unit and made sure everything was packed neatly in it. Bob paid the movers and the manager of the storage unit for three months storage. They then came back to the trailer with a large pizza. They sat around on the mattress eating the pizza when George hobbled in on crutches.

"Where have you been?" Sandy said angrily.

"I eh...fell at work and broke my leg. I have been in the hospital. They wouldn't release me, and I told them to call you, but they couldn't call you because the phone isn't working."

"Everything has been moved but this mattress and these blankets to a storage unit and the children and I are going to the Women's Shelter in the morning?" said Sandy in a matter-of-fact tone of voice. "You know what I told you about us getting back together.

You must go to rehab, have a job, and prove to me that you are not using. I never want to be in this situation ever again, do you understand me."

"Yes," George said in an angry voice.

"We will leave you to clean this place up for your relative. Sandy and the children are going to a hotel tonight to get a hot meal and  warm bed." Bob said as he grabbed the suitcases Sandy had gotten ready to go to the shelter with. He stomped out of the trailer gritting his teeth. He angrily tossed the suitcases into the back of his van. He was so angry, he wanted to punch George. How could he do this to his family? Bob wondered as everyone followed him to the van. Sandy got all the children into to their car seats and told them to wave at their father as Bob started the van and drove out of the lane. They left George standing on the step of the trailer watching them leave.

Bob took them to a pharmacy where Sandy got the children vitamins, cough syrup, aspirins, and Vicks for the children's colds. They then headed to the large hotel where they got a large suite for all of them to stay the night. They proceeded to bathe all the children in hot water and get them in clean, warm, one-piece pajamas with Vicks on their chests and medicine in their bellies. Then Sandy took a long hot bath while Bob and Lynda watched television with the children sitting on their laps being cuddled in warm blankets. When Sandy got dressed and came to watch television with the family. They ordered room service and soon were eating hot meals. The children were getting tired and soon the three of them were curled up together in one of the double beds sleeping soundly.

The three adults sat and talked about the situation. Sandy told them what George had told her about when he became addicted. Bob and Lynda had her parents living with them, they did not have enough room to take Sandy and the children back to their small house. Sandy said she would go into the Women's Shelter, while Bob and Lynda would try to find an apartment in their town three hours away. They wanted her near them, so they could help her. Lynda knew what her daughter was going through because her first husband had left her with three children to raise on her own. They were older than Sandy's children which was easier than what Sandy faced with three children under the age of four.

The next morning, after they had a large breakfast, Bob and Lynda watched as Sandy and the children with their three suitcases and their car seats entered the Women's Shelter. Lynda and Bob felt terrible leaving them there, but they had a job to do. Bob knew a lot of people so when he got home, he started looking for an apartment for his daughter.

# CHAPTER 4

A few weeks later, an apartment was found with Bob guaranteeing that the rent would be paid on time. The movers had come with Sandy's belongs. She told them which room she wanted each item in and it did not take her long to get the apartment organized. She was an expert at moving thanks to George. She was emptying the last box of children's toys when there was a knock on her door. She opened the door and saw George standing there.

"What ah…are you doing here?" Sandy asked with surprise in her voice.

"I bribed the storage locker owner to call me when your locker was being emptied. I followed the moving van here." "You are not staying here."

"Sandy, I promise I won't use again."

"You are not getting out of going to a rehab center so you can stop your begging now."

"I came to see you and the children before I go into the rehab center here in town." George said. "I am going to prove to you that I am going to stop using for you and the children."

"Things are going to be different. When I was in the shelter, I talked to counsellors, and they told me to keep you on an allowance. You will not have money to buy drugs. All drugs in the house will be under lock and key. You will have to ask me for any medication or extra money you want," Sandy stated firmly.

"Isn't that getting a little extreme. If I earn the money, I should be able to spend some money on what I want."

"No, you will be living by my rules if you want your family back," Sandy said trying to keep her voice stern to let George know she was going to stick to these rules. "If you want something you need to ask me if you can get it and we will go together to get the item."

"I am a grown man. I shouldn't need to ask you for a pack of cigarettes or a tool for work."

"You will have your allowance for those things unless it is a big item." Sandy said firmly.

"I am going to prove to you that I can be drug free. I have cut my use in half for the last week. Just wait and see, I will be drug free soon. I am to go into rehab today in town here."

"Why here? There is a rehab center in the building that our doctor was in when I was with you."

"I wanted to be near you so you and the children can visit me and remind me what I will be fighting for. I will leave the van with you. Can I see the children?"

"They have been asking about you. They don't know what is going on?"

"Daddy," Patricia yelled when she saw her father step through the door. She ran to him and gave him a hug. Tammy followed behind her and got her hug from her father. He went into the living room and picked up his five-month-old son and held him close. Buddy looked up at his father with a big smile on his face. They were soon on the floor playing and laughing with their father who was enjoying every minute with them. While Sandy sat nearby wondering if they would ever be a family again.

George went into the rehab center for the next two months. Both Sandy and George had counselling during this time. Sandy took classes on how to tell if an addict was using again. She had a problem George was acting the same as he did when she knew he was using.

How would she tell when and if he went back to using drugs? He was a master at lying and manipulation. This scared her. Could she trust him? She did not know if she could or not but if she wanted to keep her family together, she would have to give him a chance. She knew he had always gone to work even when he was hurting, and he was a good father. She hoped he was strong enough to get through the ordeal he was facing.

When George got out of the rehab center, he did not return to his hometown. Instead, he rented a room in a lady's house three blocks away from Sandy's apartment. He also got a job at a construction company in town, so he could be near his family. He visited them daily.

She was finding it hard to live on the third floor with three young children. If she got groceries, she needed help to get the groceries and the three children upstairs. If she got the children up the stairs, she needed someone to stay with the children while she got the groceries from the first floor. Doing the laundry presented the same problem. Her mother and father both worked so she could not get them to help her that often.

George made sure that he came to her rescue and helped her with these chores.     In exchange, she had to listen to his pleadings for her to take him back. Every night she heard him preach to her that she could not raise the children on her own.

She had to watch every penny she spent to make ends meet. He had got a job at a construction company and was making good money, but he was not paying her child support. When she asked him for money to pay for something she needed for the family, he would tell her that she could not support the children without him. She began to believe him.

The other problem was that the lady in the apartment below them worked nights and slept during the day. She kept complaining to the superintendent who kept warning Sandy that she needed to keep the children quiet during the day. For three children under the age of four, this was a challenge.

In the meantime, George started telling Sandy things like his landlady had started going through his belongings. Then he told her another story of how he found the landlady in his room smelling one of his shirts. This made him feel uncomfortable. This went on for months as he told her story after story of the landlady's advances. As he tried to convince Sandy to take him back. Eventually, George moved out of her landlady's home saying the landlady had climbed into his bed with him.

He started sleeping in the van. It was fall and the weather was getting colder. This played on Sandy's conscience since she remembered how cold she had been in the trailer with some heat.

George did not have any heat. She found out much later from Tyler, a man that he worked with, that he had offered George, a place to stay but George refused because he knew that sleeping in the van would play on Sandy's emotions and she would take him back. She had been manipulated by George again.

Seven months later, Bob had met George's landlady at a party.

Bob learned that George had been kicked out of her home when he was caught stealing her pain killers. Sandy had already let George back into her home because she had felt sorry for him. It took a week of debating with himself before Bob told Sandy what he had learned. She told her dad that addicts sometimes relapse and she would deal with George. Sandy and George had a huge argument about his lying to her and his trying to steal the lady's pain killers. George again made a promise that he would not use ever again. While Sandy became more and more watchful and suspicious of George.

# CHAPTER 5

When the lease of the apartment was up, George found them a small house to rent that was perfect for Sandy. Everything was on the main floor except the bedrooms, and it was an open concept, so she could watch the children while she worked around the house. The school bus for the children stopped right in front of the house. She could easily take the three children out the door and across the street to get the girls on and off the school bus. There was also a large park nearby that she took the children to. She loved to watch them run and play.

Sandy set up the bank so when George's pay came into the bank. They would transfer all his wages to her private account. Sandy would put one hundred dollars into George's account. She paid all the bills on time, and they were starting to have financial security. She bought a lock box with a combination lock to keep any drugs in the house and her debit card out of his reach. This irritated George. He thought that he should be able to spend the money he worked for on anything he wanted without having to ask permission. He was continually trying to get extra money out of Sandy. She knew that he had enough money in his account to pay for coffees, cigarettes, and gas. The idea of him begging for money slowly caused George to recent Sandy for keeping him on this regiment. Sandy kept telling him that she was only doing what the counsellor had told her to do.

Everything seemed to be going fine other than George complaining about the allowance he had to live on. Until he was fired from his job because a compressor disappeared from his job site.

Sandy wondered if George had taken it to buy drugs, but she could not find any drugs in the house or the van. The counsellors had told her not to accuse him unless she had solid proof. George told Sandy that it was Tyler Collins who worked with George on several jobs. She did not know what to think. She had committed herself to save her marriage if she could and help her husband defeat his addiction, but she was finding it extremely stressful.

What added to the stress was Buddy, her son. He was not developing the way the girls had. He preferred playing alone. He would only eat things like cereal, hot dogs, cheese, and crackers. He would have tantrums if one of the other children took one of his toys out of the position, he had put it in. He preferred playing alone. She was also having a hard time with his toilet training. She had no idea what was wrong with him but there was something. Even the doctor could not tell her what was the matter with the child?

When Buddy started pre-kindergarten that September, his teacher noticed that Brody showed signs of autism. Sandy was informed of the teacher's concern. Sandy had Buddy tested. He was diagnosed with high functioning Asperger's. Sandy now had the challenge of helping her son overcome his disabilities added to the load she was already carrying. She learned everything she could about Buddy's condition and started working with him to overcome his social awkwardness. She also found that loud noises, strong lights, frustration, and a lot of social interaction could send Buddy into a tantrum. Buddy was having screaming, kicking, and hitting tantrums almost daily. She would have to go to the school to calm him down.

Until Patricia learned how to settle her brother down. The teacher would call her from her class, and she would sit with Buddy talking to him and helping him with the thing that had set him off.

George found a new job which paid him more and he really enjoyed the work he was doing. For the first time in a long time, George seemed happy. When Sandy learned that his company was setting up a retirement fund up for their employees, she felt that they were finally starting to get financially secure. They wanted George to get a money order for seven hundred dollars and they were going to match the amount to set up his fund. Sandy scraped up the money. She went in with him to make sure the boss got the money order. She got the money order out of her purse and handed it to George who put it on the desk in front of his boss. The boss slid the corner of it under the paperweight that sat on his desk. They sat and talked a bit before Sandy and George left the room.

The boss went to put the money order into his desk drawer, and it had disappeared. He searched all over and could not find it. He had not seen anyone touch it. Where had it gone? They never did find it and Sandy wondered if George had swiped it when they were not looking. She had no proof and George was already grumpy because of the money allowance he was living on. She just watched him in the next few weeks trying to determine if he was on a drug or not, but he acted the same as usual. She searched the house and the car but didn't find anything. The idea of George using was on Sandy's mind continually.

Eight months later, Sandy's grandmother died leaving her a large sum of money. All she wanted was a home for her and her children, so they would never have to move again. Sandy wanted to buy a house, but she learned that their bankruptcy from years before had never been finalized. She was upset with George because that was one of the things that he had supposed paid to have done. Until it was, they could not own a place of their own. Sandy asked her parents if they would buy the house in their name. Her parents did not have the income to support another mortgage. They used George's income and Sandy promised that they would pay all the expenses for the house. Sandy legally was just renting the house from her parents. When her parents agree they started looking at places.

Two days later, they found a three-bedroom bungalow. It was owned by Tyler Collins. The man that George worked with. He was selling it because he was going through a nasty breakup with his common-law wife. When Sandy's parents were taken to see the house before they bought it, they were concerned at how small the two children's bedrooms were. George told them that he planned to add onto the house and make larger bedrooms for the children. He also told them that Tyler was willing to sell the house at a lower price if George bought it right away. When Sandy's parents went to see their lawyer about the purchase of the house. Their lawyer said that he could not represent them because he was representing Tyler in a nasty breakup from his common-law wife.

The day that the sale of the house was to be completed. The lawyer that had been recommended to them almost vetoed the sale. He said that he did not like what was going on with the seller's side of the sale. He asked Bob and Lynda if we knew anything about this.

They did not since they had only met Tyler once when they were shown the house. The lawyer let the sale go through. They later learned that Tyler had made over one hundred thousand dollars on the sale of the house and his common-in-law wife never got a cent from the house.

Sandy was in heaven. She finally had a home that she could raise her children in and never move again. She loved that house. She rearranged the furniture several times until she found the perfect place for each piece of furniture. She painted the walls and redecorated each room.

At first George showed a lot of pride in the house and spent time landscaping the place. He brought large equipment in from a rental place to remove unwanted dead trees and made a path through the four acres of land to the river that ran through the back of his property. He set a trampoline up for the children and built steps up to it for them and a net around it to keep them safe from falling off it. He also built them a slide, swing set with a climbing ramp and a club house. They even bought a small pool for the children to learn to swim in.

Everything seemed to be going good for them. George got a promotion, the children were doing good in school, and Sandy was feeling better about everything in her life and most of all George seemed to truly be drug free. At least there was no missing money, and all their bills were paid.

Until their world was turned upside down when George had an accident at work. He was standing on the tenth rung of a tall twelve- foot ladder when the rung broke. He landed on his feet jarring his back. He started having a lot of pain. He was sent to the hospital. An x-ray showed that George had broken his back before in several places from the first accident. This time he had cracked several vertebrae.

The cracked vertebrae slipped down over the vertebrae below them. He needed surgery and pain killers.

The doctor put George on a medical leave and set up an appointment with a surgeon. George signed a pain contract with the doctor who was told by George that Sandy would supervise the dosage of pain killers he would be taking because of his past addiction. When he got home, he told Sandy that he needed surgery, and he would have to be extremely careful. She did not know a thing about the drugs, until her phone dropped down between the front seat of the van and the console two days later. She went ballistic when she pulled a prescription bottle of pain killers from under the seat.

She called the doctor and started yelling at the doctor about putting George back on pain killers that he had been addicted to. When she stopped to take a breath, the doctor broke into the conversation telling her that right now George needed those pills. He also explained that after the surgery, they would wean George off the pain killers. This stressed Sandy out because she did not want to go through George's rehab again.

A few weeks later, George was fired from his job. The company had been bought by a bigger construction company. The new manager had gone over all the personal files, and he spotted a problem with George's work file. He had used the company gas card a lot to not only fill his company truck but to fill his personal vehicle and other people's vehicles on a regular basis. He had also used rented equipment on his own property and charged the rental cost to a job he had been supervising.

When Sandy heard this, she knew then that George had been lying to her about not using drugs all this time. She now had some decisions to make. Did she want to stay with George if he was going to be using drugs? They now were on unemployment that took 6 weeks to get a cheque and George had lost his benefits which were paying for his pain killers. Would they be able to make ends meet and keep their home? Would he ever be able to get a job again with two incidents on his records that he misused company resources.

This sent Sandy into a deeper depression as she worried herself sick on how she would cope with George addicted again and how they would keep the house she loved. She did not want to ever have to move her children again. If they broke up, could she keep her house and support the children. George kept telling her that she needed him to support them. She was also coping with Buddy having tantrums at school and being called by the teacher to come to the school. The doctor ended up putting her on an anti-depressant to help her cope with the stress and depression she was coping with.

George was told by the surgeon that if a problem occurred during the operation he might end up in a wheelchair for the rest of his life. This scared Sandy. George was ready to take the chance because he was in so much pain. What would happen if he were permanently disabled?

They decided to visit George's family and bring them the news of what he would be facing if the surgery went wrong. Their sixteen- year-old van broke down a few blocks from his uncle's place. His uncle repaired old cars to supplement his pension. They towed it to his house and Sandy was told that the transmission had gone in it. They          did not have the money for a new transmission or the money to tow it three-hours back home. George gave it to his uncle for parts. He later confessed to Sandy that he gave the van to his uncle in exchange for drugs.

George's brother drove them home. Leaving them stranded with no vehicle fifteen miles from town. Sandy could not even get milk for her children when they ran out. Sandy called Bob who took her out car shopping. They found a cheap old car that Sandy could afford.

# CHAPTER 6

Sandy could not understand why George was using but she could not understand why he could not see that the cost of his addiction which was growing at an alarming rate, was destroying his family. She was so desperate to understand why he would give up everything they had for the next dose of pills. She even tried some drugs just to see what George saw in them, but she did not like the effect they had on her.

With the hope of George being drug free in the future like the doctor had promised, she stayed with him. To save her family and her home, Sandy stepped up and got a job selling cars at a large dealership in town. They gave her a demo car to drive. She only had a few items in her closet that was dressy enough for selling cars and that still fit her after having three children in four years. She wore jeans and t-shirts since she moved in with George. She bought a new wardrobe of dresses and pant suits at the resale shops in town. George became jealous seeing her dress up to work with all the men at the dealership.

He also was angry that he was not allowed to drive her demo car. Instead, he had to drive the cheap old car that Sandy had bought a month before she got the job. He was so upset by this that he got an under-the-table job where he made four-thousand dollars. He took the old car and the money and got himself a truck to drive around in.

His injury turned George into a stay-at-home dad. The problem was that he did not do any of the work that a stay-at-home mom does. He left all the dishes, washing, cleaning, and mopping for Sandy to do. He even got to the point that he did not even take the garbage to the road for pick up. Instead, he piled it into trailers parked just out the front door. He told Sandy that he would take the garbage to the dump when he got money to pay for the dump fee. When the trailers were filled, he started to pile the garbage against the house fifteen feet from the back door of the house. Rats and mice moved into the garbage heaped within feet of where the children played but George did not care.

He had to watch the two younger children because they were going to school every other day. They spent a lot of time in his truck. He started picking up things from the side of the road. He also visited job sites and picked things out of the dumpsters like scrap windows and steel. He piled these items in the back yard telling Sandy he was going to use them on the shed he wanted or fix them up to sell. But he never touched them. The yard was beginning to look like a junk yard.

He built the children a shelter at the end of the driveway to use while they were waiting for the school bus in the winter. He used scrapes of things that he had laying around in the yard. He did not secure the shelter to the ground and used a basic wood box frame with sheet metal sides. He put a window as the roof which had a crack in the glass. He put another window in the side of the structure, so they could see the bus coming down the road. Unfortunately, it was so wobbly that Sandy was scared that the glass on the roof would shatter and shower the children in glass if the children bumped into the shelter walls. Sandy would not allow them to use it which made George angry.

George was doing things that upset her. Like when the heating system needed a small repair. George called the repairman who came and fixed the unit, but he did not pay for it. He told the man that he did not own the house Bob did. He never told Sandy or Bob about the repair, and it went to the credit bureau. When Bob found out about it, he paid for it immediately, but he was furious that George had done this. Sandy was livid, because George had broken the promise that they would pay all the bills for the house. This caused a huge argument which made George even more angry with Sandy. He would not accept that she was doing these things to keep a roof over their children's heads, food on the table, and getting him drug free again.

The day of the operation finally arrived. The hospital was a four- hour drive away. They had left the day before. Sandy got a hotel room near the hospital and George was admitted to the hospital that night.

The surgery went well but Sandy could not afford to stay more than a few days at the hotel. She had to get back to the children and her job. George was angry that she would not stay with him all the time he was in the hospital. He felt that she was abandoning him, so she could go back to her job because she was looking for a man, so she could ditch him.

When the doctor informed her that George could not be sent home unless he had a lift-chair that had adjustable positions she did not know what to do. She could not afford the chair and she could not afford staying in a hotel to make George happy.

When Bob heard about what the doctor had said, he came to her rescue. He went out and bought the chair and got it delivered to her house. He figured that after George was done using it, he could bring it back to his house for his mother who had a bad back.

Sandy came home one day to find the chair was gone.

"Where is your chair? Don't you need it yet to get up and to support your back," Sandy said.

"The mechanism broke on it. I called the company, and they took it to be repaired," George said.

"How did you break it?"

"I didn't. I found the children playing with the control and bouncing on the chair. I told them it wasn't a play toy, but they don't listen to me," George said angrily. "I must go and get cigarettes and milk. I will be back in a little while."

"Why didn't you call me, I could have picked those items up on my way home."

"I did call but you were busy having a meeting with one of your men friends."

"Don't start, I am not having an affair with anyone."

"Yes, that is what you keep telling me but that doesn't mean I have to believe you. Especially when you dress so sexy all the time."

"I am not wearing anything trashy that shows anything." Sandy said firmly. "What is wrong with the dresses, skirts, and pant suits that I wear. What is your problem? I am with you aren't I." Sandy said as she wondered why George was so jealous.

"Are you?" George said. "You never dressed in skirts above your knees and blouses that show your cleavage for me."

"You rarely take me out, so I dress appropriately for a stay-at-home mom in jeans and tee shirts." Sandy said angrily. "Besides the style now is to have your skirts above your knee by an inch or two and when it comes to most of my blouses, I don't show any cleavage. Grow up."

"You do every time you bend over a desk in front of a man," as George slammed the front door as he walked out.

Sandy thought about what George said. She stood in front of the bathroom mirror and bent forward. She did show a little bit of cleavage. She realized that this happened to every woman, and she was not showing more than an inch of cleavage. Why was George so jealous? She had not done anything that was different than any working woman who works in an office. This stressed her out more.

Two months later the chair had not reappeared. Lynda and Bob were wondering what was going on with it. Sandy finally learned that George had sold the chair for two hundred dollars. This infuriated Bob because he had paid over a thousand dollars for it.

Bob decided to get some of his money back for the chair. He asked George to do some light work around his house that needed to be done. He needed a sturdy railing on the side steps built, so his mother had something to lean on as she went up and down the steps. He also had a bedroom that needed painting.

George showed up to do the work. He built the railing in a few hours. He went in to get a drink of water which he got but he also went into the cupboard by the sink which was where Bob's mother kept her pain killers. She had been on morphine for years. She was so careful using it that she counted the number in the bottle every day to make sure that she did not accidently take an extra dose. The next morning, she was five pills short.

The pharmacy was also extremely careful with the morphine. Bob's mother tried to order her pills five days earlier than usual to make up for the pills that had disappeared. The pharmacy refused to give her the pills until the date that she normally would run out. She had been on morphine for over twenty years so going five days without pills sent this eighty-four-year-old lady into withdrawal and severe pain.

This infuriated Bob and Lynda. George never came back into their house again. Sandy came in and finished painting the railing and the bedroom to help pay for the chair that George had sold.

She was furious about what he did to her grandmother. George taking the pills added to the tension between them.

His drug use was now out in the open and he began selling anything they owned to get money for the drugs. Sandy wanted to leave him but who would babysit the two younger kids. Could she  make enough to support her and the children? Right now, every penny she was making was spent keeping their bills paid, food on the table and his medical expenses.

# CHAPTER 7

Sandy was frantically searching for her wedding ring one morning. She had taken it off when she was scrubbing a dirty burnt casserole pan the night before. She had forgotten to put it back on. She had spent hours searching for it after she realized it was not on her finger the next morning. She was scared to tell George she had thought it was in the drain.

George laughed at her. "I found it last night on the counter, so I took it. I traded it for drugs."

"Why would you do that?" Sandy said angrily.

"You want someone else so let him buy you jewellery," George said as he walked out the door and jumped in his truck and left.

George went over the edge when Sandy started going to play euchre every Monday night just to get away from the stress of a full- time job, doing all the housework, and a husband that was getting more and more miserable to live with. She went with her parents who had learned about the euchre club from one of the men she worked with.

When George learned that some of the men, she worked with was there, he accused her of having an affair.

A month later they were at home working on the flower bed, when one of the children let it slip that their father has been setting up play dates for them. The child also mentioned that her father had kissed a lady in the park while they were playing on the swing set.

Sandy started yelling at him for his infidelity. He got violent with Sandy hitting her several times, giving her a concussion, dragging her by the hair around the yard threatening her the whole time. Until finally he dragged her to the small pond at the side of the house and tried to drown her.

He held her head face down in the water. She could feel her lungs screaming for air and she felt like she was going to black out soon. Her only hope was to act like she was dead. She did and he loosened his grip on her and started backing away from her. He thought she was dead, and he was stunned that he had murdered her. She suddenly sprang up and ran out of the pond coughing and sputtering as she screamed for Patricia to call the police. The neighbours heard the children screaming that he was hurting their mother. They called the police and a ten minutes later the police pulled into the yard. They found the neighbour boys holding George who was screaming threats at Sandy as she stood shaking with a blanket wrapped around her.

The children were shaking and crying. They had heard the threats that their father had screamed at their mother. He threated that he would come one night and get the children out of the house before he set the house on fire with their mother inside it. They were traumatized by this threat. He threatened that he would make her lose her job, lose her house, and lose her children.

The police charged him with assault and jailed him. Sandy started divorce proceedings immediately. She was scared to death of him and wanted him out of her life. She had tried to keep their marriage going. But George's need for drugs and jealousy won out.

The divorce came though quickly with a peace bond attached. He was only able to see the children with supervision. He was ordered to pay child support and half of their baby-sitting cost, school activities and medical expenses. The judge also ordered him to pay the court costs. George ignored the court's orders. He did however start his campaign to carry out his threat to make her lose her job, make her lose her home, and make her lose her children.

Sandy tried to get FRO to help her get the child support that George was not paying her. Sandy would find out where George was working. FRO would start the process of garnishing his wages. As soon as he found out that they had found him, he would quit the job and go out looking for a new job. They never tried to take his driver's license or construction tickets.

George however knew where she worked so he started causing her trouble. He began calling every man she worked with and accusing them of having an affair with his ex-wife. When that did not get her fired, he proceeded to call the men's wives and told them that their husbands were having an affair with Sandy. This caused her trouble until one of the ladies asked George, what day were they together. The date he gave the lady was a weekend when she and her husband were out of town visiting their family. She told everyone involved that he was lying about Sandy having an affair with one of the men.

George and his mother were found unfit by the court to have custody of the children. They did not want to accept this ruling. They started a campaign with CAS to prove to them that Sandy was an unfit mother. They would call CAS and accused Sandy of doing something wrong. A CAS worker would come to her home and open a file. They made sure that the children were eating, had clothes to wear and were going to school and were healthy. They would then close the case until the next accusation was called in against Sandy.

In the meantime, Sandy was not sleeping well, she felt like the house was being watched. She also felt a few times that someone had been in the house while they were away. She was scared to be there alone with the children. Even Lynda felt like the house was being watched when she babysat for Sandy.

Every morning she was reminded of the threat and the near drowning. She would wake up to find all three children in bed with her. They were scared that their father would come in the middle of the night and take them from the house before they could wake their mother. They figured that if they were in bed with her, they would be able to wake her before their father burnt the house done with her in it like he had threatened.

She went to see the mental health doctor about a class for Buddy. He saw how stressed she was. She sat the whole time biting her nails and her leg bouncing. He put her through some tests and discovered she was suffering with ADHD (attention deficit hyperactivity disorder) and PTSS (post traumatic stress syndrome). The doctor put her on Ritalin. The medical name for this drug is methylphenidate which is a central nervous system stimulant. This is the standard drug used for ADHD. When George learned that the medicine, she was on contained Meth. He called everyone they knew and told them that Sandy was using meth.

CAS was demanding that Sandy take the children for complete medical exams because of the complains George and his mother were making. She had to set up appointments for all their shots, hearing tests, eye tests, physical exams, and dental exams. She also had to start taking blood tests for the court before she got sole custody of her children.

Each appointment took her away from work which mean less money because she was working on commission. She also was using all her benefits up which she had just received from her company. She was struggling to pay for babysitting for three children over the summer vacation. George was supposed to help pay for half of this but      like usual he was a deadbeat dad.

She began suffering with an abscessed tooth which she had a history having. She could not go to the dentist because she had no benefits left and she had no extra money to pay him. She was living on Tylenol to ease the pain. Unfortunately, the abscess turned into blood poisoning. She lost a lot of weighs in a short period of time. This added to the rumor that was going around that she was addicted to meth. She finally went to the hospital, and they put her on intravenous antibiotics every night for a week to clean up the infection, but they did not pull the tooth.

In the meantime, Sandy was tormented by George and his mother who were calling the children and telling them that they were going to take them to Disneyland and other fun places. They told them they were going to live with their father because their mother was unfit to raise them and all kinds of other lies.

George and his mother encouraged the children to do things to cause Sandy problems at the school or with CAS. They promised the children toys if they did cause trouble for their mother. On one occasion, one of the children told a lie to get the toy promised, but their father or grandmother never got the child that toy. Another time, they encouraged one of the children to unpack the lunch their mother had packed for them. The child did what she had been told to do by repacking her lunch with candy and treats. What child would refuse to do this? She was following her father's instructions, so she thought it was alright. Of course, this led to another CAS investigation.

George and his mother had their visits with the children at the visitation center, they would bring them dollar toys and sometimes clothes. Which was fine with Sandy, but they would try the new clothes on the children at the center and throw the clothes they came in into the garbage there.

This angered Sandy especially when they threw out things like Buddy's one hundred-dollar boots. Sandy had laid out that kind of money for his boots because they had two loops one on each side to make them easy to pull on. They had helped cut down the number of tantrums that Buddy was having at school. They replaced them with regular laced up boots. They did not know or care that Sandy had to spend the next few nights showing Buddy how to loosen the boots to get his feet in easily and then how to tie them back up with a bow.

They did not care about the number of tantrums that Brody was having at school.

When Sandy asked the ladies that worked at the visitation center to get the boots for her. They refused to so she asked if she could go up and get them. The answer was no so Sandy started dressing the children in their oldest clothes to see their father, so she did not lose any of their good clothes.

Of course, the women at the visitation center reported this to CAS and Sandy was chastised for this. CAS would not listen to the fact that their good clothes were being thrown out.

Sandy finally got angry when her boss came in and started hassling her about the number of hours, she was taking off work. because of all the appointments, the trips to the nearby school, and leaving early to get the children from their babysitter.

She looked at her boss and said, "I know that I have taken time off for my divorce, my custody battle to get my children, and the CAS appointments my ex has caused. Yet I am one of your top salespersons, but I have had it with the rumors and looks I get from my workmates. who just assume that my ex-husband is telling the truth. I lost weight because I had blood poisoning. No one asked they just assumed George was telling the truth. I quit," she said as she handed over the keys to her demo car. She packed up her belongings and went across the street to another car dealership.

When she told them who she was and that she was looking for a car. She was hired on the spot because of her reputation of being on the top sellers list every month.

Sandy was being judged by everyone with out hearing the facts. The teachers at the school were judging her because she did not have the money for some of the trips and pizza days that they were putting on for the children. The people she had worked with at the first car dealership had assumed she was using without knowing about the abscessed tooth. No one asked for the truth they only assumed that the rumors were correct and whispered behind her back instead of asking what was going on with her.

George had accomplished his first threat that she would lose her job. He had not expected her to get a new job that quickly. In fact, it was a good move for Sandy because George did not know any of the people she was now working with. He could not call and make trouble for her. It reduced the stress she had been under.

# CHAPTER 8

Sandy tried for one year to keep the home she loved but finally her fear won out. The home invasions, the feeling she was being watched, the messy yard and all George's calls and accusations were stressing her out. She talked with her parents about selling the place and her buying a house on her own where George would not know where she was. They agreed that this was a good move, so Sandy started preparing to put her home up for sale.

Bob had the biggest dumpster the company had dropped on her front lawn. Her parents and a few friends came over and they started filling the dumpster. They first started with the rat-infested garbage that was piled up in the trailers and then the pile that was against the back of the house.

The school shelter came down next when Bob bumped into it. He was showered with glass as the cracked window shattered into thousands and thousands of tiny pieces. It took two days of backbreaking work to pick up all the lose metal, bed springs, broken toys, windows, and other things that George had collected and dropped all over the property.

That first night of the cleanup, Sandy got a phone call that spurred her to find a new place as quickly as she could.

"Hello," Sandy said.

"Hello, my name is Larry. Is George there?"

"No, he doesn't live here anymore. We are divorced." Sandy said as she wondered what this call was about.

"He has my trailer and he owe me some money. I want to get in touch with him,"

Sandy had a funny feeling. "I don't know where he is. I have a peace bond against him, and he will be charged with trespassing if he comes on the property." Sandy told the man in a shaky voice.

"Do you know where he might be."

"No, I haven't seen him. You mentioned a trailer. I have two in my front yard behind the trees at the road. I will be moving, and I have no use for them. If one of them is yours, you are welcome to come and get it." Sandy was glad that they had got the truck trailers cleaned out and washed down.

"You are moving? Have you sold the place?"

"Not yet," Sandy wondered why this man was so interested if her place was sold or not.

"Good, Good, I might get my money back then."

"What do you mean?" Sandy questioned.

"Well, if you are selling then George will get some money and he will be able to pay me."

"Does he owe you for drugs?" "Yes."

"When the house sells, he won't get a penny from it." Sandy said.

"What do you mean? He owns it doesn't he."

"No, my parents own it. We could not buy it because of a bankruptcy so my parents bought it in their name for us. We paid all the bills for it but legally we were just renting from them."

"He told me and my friends that he was going to force you to sell so he could get money to pay us."

"He is not going to get a cent and he has no right to any part of this property. He is trespassing if he comes on the property,"

"We have seen him there often while you are away."

"You have seen him around the house," questioned Sandy.

"Yes, he has entered it by the window several times."

"I though I was just imagining that someone had been in the house when we were gone." Sandy said.

"I have had people watching the house for awhile now," said the man. "We thought you were still with the scumbag. I will make sure you are left alone, and he won't get in your house again."

"I appreciate that, but I will be moving. My children are so scared that he is going to carry out his threat of burning the house down around me that they will not sleep in their own beds. Instead, they are climbing in bed with me every night. For all our sakes, I am giving up the house I love."

"Sorry to hear that but I will make sure that he backs off and leaves you alone when I find him," Larry said. "I will come and get the trailer in the next few days. I will make sure that you and the children are not there."

"Thank you," Sandy listed the house the next morning.

George had accomplished his second threat to make her lose her house. He just didn't expect not to get anything out of it. He felt Sandy, and her parents had swindled him out of the money that he had paid into the house when Larry explained to him that he legally never bought the place. This angered him and he wanted revenge.

Sandy found a four-bedroom house that she could afford, and a buyer for her old house. The new place was perfect. It was in a small subdivision out in the country. Her house had a stream running through the back of her property. On the other side of the stream was a hill. This made her feel safe because there was no place that people could sit and spy on her without being noticed by her. Her new neighbours were close enough if she ever needed help.

The children did not even have to change schools. Their bus picked them up just down the street from their house. She also was closer to her work. Her parents gave her all the equity in the house since most of it had been her inheritance from her grandmother, this allowed her to buy the new house in her name only.

She was feeling good about herself. She was on a strict budget, but she was able to provide for her children without help from her deadbeat husband.

Sandy and Tyler met at a wedding and started to date. They enjoyed each other' company. Tyler proposed to her one month after they met called love-bombing. Sandy said yes but she would not set a date. This upset Tyler because he was afraid, she would meet someone else at her work.

Lynda. and Bob finally got a chance to meet Tyler when they went to Buddy's birthday party. Sandy and her parents had pooled their money and bought Buddy a bigger bike for his birthday. Bob had laid it down in the back of his van. When they arrived at Sandy's house, Bob asked Buddy to help him unload the van. When the back door of the van opened and Buddy saw the bike, a huge smile spread across his face. Bob lifted it out of the van and Buddy jumped on it and began riding it around the yard yelling, "Thank you, thank you."

Ivan, Tyler's boy, was there and immediately started putting down the bike. He was yelling out to Buddy things like his bike was more expensive, his had wider wheels for dirt biking, and his was a nicer colour. Lynda classified Ivan under the heading of a spoilt, jealous child. Tyler did not say one word about his child's actions.

Then when they were all sitting on the back-porch, Tyler started showing his true colours. He began to name drop. He was friends or related to every well-known people in the city. His whole conversation kept returning to him. Sandy's parents also smelt the scent of marijuana on him. They were not impressed by him at all,

The biggest problem was that Tyler treated her children differently than he treated Ivan. Sandy had a rule that the children on a school night had to be in bed by nine o'clock. Ivan did not have any rules.

Ivan asked his father if they could have a bonfire and smores after Sandy's children were heading for bed. Well, when Sandy's children heard that Ivan was going to stay up and have a treat. They wanted smores also. What child would not? Sandy agreed that they could stay up for another hour and sent them out to the fire while she got the ingredients for smores on a tray. Tyler ordered them back to bed. He did not care about their feelings which angered Sandy.

This caused a huge argument. Sandy told him that if he did not treat the children all the same there was no use trying to go on with their relationship. This angered Tyler. He loved her but Ivan was his first born and was superior to him then her children.

Tyler was not getting the construction jobs he was used to getting when he worked with his father. This caused more stress because he was wanting Sandy to have his baby, but Sandy needed to work so she could pay her mortgage payment of six hundred dollars a month. Tyler was afraid that Sandy would meet someone else at work so he promised her that he would give her that amount to pay her mortgage. When his father had a heart attack and Tyler had to move in with his parents so he could take care of his father's farm animals. He started going further in debt. He blamed her for everything that happened. In the meantime, Sandy was struggling with all the court appearances, the hospital visits and CAS visits and counselling appointments, she had to appear at.

Tyler wanted to get custody of his son. When they picked Ivan up for another weekend with his father, Ivan said he had something to show them. He pulled out a small bag of marijuana. He told them he had gotten it out of his mother's coat. Ivan said she was using it again. Sandy had been told all kinds of crazy things that Tyler's ex-wife had done. This shocked Sandy because her children did not even know what the stuff was. She knew Tyler used it occasionally when he hurt from an old injury. He never used it to her knowledge in front of any of the children.

On the next visit, Ivan tells them that his mother has a large gym bag full of marijuana because she is selling it. Sandy is panicking about this boy being exposed to all this. She gets Ivan a disposable camera and tells him to take a picture of the bag.

On the next visit he returns the camera to Sandy who gets it developed and sure enough a picture of the gym bag is there with weed in it. Sandy argues with Tyler about him calling CAS. He refuses. Sandy is so upset because she also learned that Ivan can hardly read, and his father is not doing anything to help the boy. She finally calls CAS herself and reports Ivan's mother.

The mother proved to CAS that she did not have marijuana in her home. She also got the boy a tutor. Tyler was frustrated because he did not get custody of his son.

Six months later, Tyler told Sandy that he grew marijuana on different family members property and in his house he had owned. Sandy began wondering at that point if Tyler had set her up to call CAS so he could get custody of his son. She wondered if the marijuana in that bag was his and not his ex-wife's.

This is called gaslighting. A narcistic person will manipulate, use emotional abuse, lying, spinning the truth, and distorting your reality to get their way. Tyler starts preparing for his son to move in with them by turning part of a large mud room into a bedroom for him. It was never completed because Tyler never got custody of his son.

George turned to Tyler for help to get his children. George told him that if they could get Sandy charged with assault and she went to jail then he could get his children. Tyler was reluctant until George threatened to tell Tyler's ex-wife about the money Tyler cheated her out of when he sold the house to Sandy's parents.

Sandy had had it with George and her ex-mother-in-law, Delores, who every week caused trouble with the children, CAS, or the school. It got so bad that she finally requested that George's mother was not allowed in the visitation center. This angered Delores.

The next week, Delores drove her son to the visitation center but instead of parking in front of the building like she was supposed to.

She parked in the apartment building parking lot next door so she could see the children getting out of the car to go inside.

When Sandy and Tyler pulled in to let the children go in. Delores started yelling and waving at the children. Once the children were in the building Tyler drove out of the parking lot and headed to the grocery store which they did every Sunday. On the way there, Sandy spotted Delores' car following them.

Tyler parked the car as Sandy got ready to climb out. Delores pulled up and parked a few cars away from them. Delores climbed out of the car with a large coffee cup in each hand holding them like they were filled with hot coffee.

Delores called to her," May I talk to you for a few minutes?"

"Ok," Sandy said hoping that she could settle the problem she was having with her ex-mother-in-law."

"Why are you not letting my son see his children whenever he wants to."

"I am not the one who set those rules up. The court did." "He is a good father who loves his children."

"If he loves them why not pay the child support, he owes me. He is depriving his children of things that other fathers give to their children."

"Like what, he has been bringing them clothes and toys," Delores answered.

"Is the amount of money that he is spending equal to six hundred dollars a month?"

"No," Delores answered. "That is outrages."

"Then he is not supporting his children the way the court thinks he should. The money is so they can have dance classes, karate, or gymnastics or other things children want to get into. It is for babysitting, medical bills and school trips."

"Why should he have to pay for babysitting so you can go out on the town with your men friends?"

"It is not for me so I can go out with friends. It is for the time that I must leave them to go to work."

"You should be home with your children not working."

"I must work to keep a house over their heads. If I was getting that child support, I could stay home with the children. He is the one who is hurting the children, not me."

"He is a good father. He should be able to see his children anytime and be able to take them places," Delores said angrily.

"The court set up the restrictions because of his actions not anything I said to them."

"He never hurt his children," Delores yelled at Sandy. "No, but he almost killed me."

"He should have then I would have my grandchildren."

"No, you wouldn't Delores. You were classified as unfit to raise your own sons. Why would the court give you custody of my children?"

"He destroyed his chances of getting the children when he made a scene at the children's school. It was so bad that the principle called in a bomb threat to get the police to the school quickly to protect the children. Your son was high on drugs at the time. He then went to the babysitters the next day. He threatened her until my mother arrived.

He backed off because he knew my mother does not take any guff from anyone. I changed babysitters the next day to protect them." "My son is not addicted to drugs," Delores yelled.

"Yes, he is," Sandy stated firmly." "You are lying," Delores yelled.

"I have had it, Delores. You do not want to see the truth. George is addicted to drugs, has not taken anger management classes the court ordered, and you both are unfit to raise children. Do not bother talking to me or my children again." Sandy said, "I am done talking to you."

"I will have custody of the children," Delores yelled as she made the motion like she was going to throw the hot coffee at Sandy.

Sandy was three months pregnant with Tyler's baby and had had a miscarriage five months before this. She did not want to lose this baby or be scalded by hot coffee. She hit the bottom of both cups which made them flight out of Delores hands spewing hot steaming coffee on the ground as the cups rolled across the parking lot by the wind.

"I am done with you, Delores. Goodbye," Sandy said as she turned and walked back to where Tyler sat in the car.

"Get me out of here, Tyler. I have had it with her."

Sandy should have reported this to the police especially when she saw Delores running up to every car who had a person in it. Sandy's PTSS and ADHD combined to make her just want to flee. This was in January.

The police did not charge Sandy with assault until March. By then the coffee cups and the spilt coffee was gone. She had no witnesses except Tyler. When Tyler was interviewed by the police, Tyler was not much help to Sandy. He did not answer the questions he was asked clearly. The police told him flat out that his testimony would be considered bias because they were living together.

This drained Sandy's finances more as she had to make more one-hour trips into the courthouse and the hours spent there waiting to be called up in front of the judge. Then when she got there, the lawyer on her ex-mother-in-law side would ask for more time and they would set another court date. This went on for over a year.

A snowstorm added to this when the roads were all closed.

Sandy called the court to find out what she should do. She was told that the court judge would reschedule the cases for that day, and she would be notified. No one called her to tell her that the session was scheduled for the next day. The next day the police showed up at her door and arrested her for missing a court appearance. This added 18 more trips to court and was settled over a year later by her paying a thirty-dollar fine. What made matters worse was that Sandy did not qualify for legal aid. She did not have money to pay for a lawyer, so she tried to defend herself, but she did not know how. This did not help her.

Sandy in the meantime was worried about losing her children if she was sent to jail or had no place to live. She was losing her house without the six hundred dollars from Tyler. FRO was not helping her get child support from George. This put a terrible strain on her pregnancy. The blood poisoning, she had, the miscarriage, and the strain made Sandy have a hard pregnancy with a lot of nausea and dizziness. This did not help the situation between them.

# CHAPTER 9

On Tyler's birthday, the children and Sandy made him a special dinner with a cake, and they decorated the house. Everything was ready for the surprize dinner, but he did not come over when he had said he would. Eventually the children when to bed upset because he had not shown up. When he did arrive, he was drunk and angry. He blamed Sandy for the large amount of debt he was in and the loss of his house in town.

Like a true narcistic person, he blamed Sandy for all his problems.

He was so angry that he started hitting her. She was seven months pregnant. He kept trying to hit her stomach, so she dropped to the floor and leaning forward using her legs and arms to protect her child. He hit her again and again. Then he grabbed her by pushing his fingers into her mouth and pulled her head back. He was so violent that he ripped one of her front teeth out of her mouth. He then grabbed her by the neck and began strangling her. He squeezed tighter and tighter. Less and less air was getting into her lungs. She realized she had to do something or her baby and her would be dead.

She mustered up all the strength that she could, and she hit him in his eye giving Tyler a shiner. He had not expected to get hit. It stunned him and he let go of her long enough for her to break the hold he had on her. She scrambled to her feet and ran into her bathroom and locked the door.

He realized what he had done. He fled from the house while she called her girl friend who told her to take pictures of her injuries. She was told to call the police, but Sandy was too scared of Tyler. She did not tell anyone of the attack until almost a year later. He messed her head up with his twisted lies and constant put downs. She thought that she had deserved to be beat up by him because her request for money was putting them both deeper and deeper into debt. Also, the fact she was having a difficult pregnancy causing her not to be able to work.

Tyler abandoned her. He went to his father's house that night and told them that Sandy was on meth and had hit him for no reason. Of course, they believed their son. His sister worked for CAS and knew how often they were called by George and others complaining about Sandy taking drugs. Now her brother confirmed that Sandy used.

Two months later Sandy went into labour. She called Lynda to come and watch the children while she was in the hospital. She also called Tyler since he was the baby's father and told him she was in labour, and she was going to the hospital.

When Lynda got to Sandy's place, they realized that neither of their cars would seat all the children and the two adults with their car seats. Sandy had no chose she had to drive herself to the hospital. Her contractions were seven minutes apart when she drove out of the driveway.

When she got there the nurses got her into one of the delivery rooms immediately. The head nurse told her that it was an extremely busy night and there was only one doctor working that night. Since she had already had three children, the nurse told her not to push until the doctor got there.

They left her in a room with no call button she could reach, no bassinette for the baby when it came, and nothing to drink or eat. She sat for over an hour with the urge to push growing stronger and stronger with every contraction.

The doctor finally came in with a nurse. They started to examine Sandy when Tyler and Ivan came into the room.

"What is Ivan doing here?" Sandy asked Tyler.

"He wants to see the baby born," said Tyler like he expected

Sandy to agree that it was a good idea.

"If I wanted an audience, I would have brought my own children not Ivan. Now get him out of here." Sandy said angrily.

"I want him to see the baby born," Tyler said. "He is staying,"

"Your wife told you she didn't want the boy here so he must leave," said the doctor as he walked into the room.

"She is not my wife, and she never will be," said Tyler angrily.

"Right now, I am concerned about your baby and your girlfriend so get that boy out of here or I will call security," said the doctor.

"This is my baby also and I want my son to see his brother born," shouted Tyler.

"You had no interest in this baby when you beat me up and abandoned me at seven months," Sandy said between gritted teeth as another strong contraction occurs.

"I am concerned with the care of this mother and her baby not with who sees the birth. She wants the child out of here so he must leave," the doctor said as he pushed a button on the wall.

A large intern came in and took the boy out to the nurse's station. As they went out of the door, Sandy finally pushed and a few minutes later a beautiful baby boy was laying on her chest. Tyler was handed the scissors and he cut the umbilical cord. The nurse took the baby and wrapped it up tightly in a blanket. She let Sandy hold it for a few minutes and then she whisked it away to be clean up and to do the tests they do on babies. While the doctor finished up taking care of Sandy.

When the nurse came back with the baby wrapped in a blanket and a little cap on his head, she handed the baby to Tyler. He held the baby until the nurse and the doctor rushed out to deliver another baby.

As soon as they left, Tyler gave the baby to Sandy and said,

"You know that this baby will never mean as much to me as Ivan does." "Then why did you push for me to have this baby?"

"I wanted to make sure you would be mine but that will never happen now." Tyler said as he walked out saying, "You are not good enough for me. I am going to take Ivan home."

Sandy was left holding the baby with no bassinette to put him in, no water to drink, no food to eat, and needing to relieve herself. She was physically and emotionally drained. Her heart was broken by Tyler's words. She cried all night as she held her baby close to her telling the baby she loved him and nursing him.

The next morning, the nurse came in to find Sandy exhausted, hungry, thirsty, and wet as she held her baby tightly.  The nurse got her cleaned up and fed. Then Sandy nursed the baby, wiped him down with a washcloth, changed his diaper, and dressed him in a sleeper and put him down for a sleep in the bassinette.

The children were anxious to meet their new brother when they arrived with their grandparents. Sandy and the children decided on the name of Carl for the baby, and each took a turn holding him and talking to him. Buddy was so excited he had written a little letter to him telling the baby how glad Buddy was to have a baby brother. They were all happy to have a new member in their family.

# CHAPTER 10

S andy had to appear in court several times for the assault case against her ex-mother-in-law. The trial date finally was here. She had been trying to represent herself, but she did not know how. The assault had occurred in January, but Sandy was charged with assault in March. By then, the coffee cups and the coffee spill were long gone before even the police got involved. She had no witnesses. Tyler had hummed and hawed when the police questioned him. He did not tell the police anything that could be used to prove that Sandy was innocent. He never mentioned the coffee cups or that Sandy had not touched Delores's arms.

Delores had one witness who did not show up and a second witness who finally admitted that she heard the argument, but she had not seen anything because her back was to them. She had been the only hope Sandy had to defend herself.

The day of the trial, Delores had got on the stand with a handkerchief dabbing her eyes crying and moaning that Sandy had been so angry that she feared for her life. She told the court that Sandy had grabbed her by her arms and shook her violently. She had bruises on her arms for weeks. If she had been injured that bad, why did she not call the police immediately and charge Sandy for assault.

Instead, she waited so she could explain the lack of bruises on her arms to the police.

When Sandy tried to tell the court about the coffee cups, Delores' lawyer objecting each time because Sandy did not have any proof of these cups ever existing.

George and his entire family were in the courtroom hoping that Sandy would be sentenced to some jail time. If she went to jail, they would go to CAS and get custody of the children transferred to their father. George's third threat would come true, and Sandy would lose her children. The judge charged her with assault but gave her two years probation instead which defeated George and his mother's plot against Sandy.

A peace bond was put into place so Sandy could not be near Delores. The peace bond backfired on George and Delores because Sandy was not allowed to be closer than one hundred yards from Delores. Sandy knew that Delores would use this against her. Sandy went to the probation officer explaining that she could not drop the children off at the visitation center or pick the children up there. If Delores parked in the apartment buildings parking lot, she would be too close to Sandy. Sandy knew that Delores would call the police and claim that Sandy broke the peace bond. George lost the right to see the children, because the peace bond prevented Sandy from going to the exchange center, but he could still call them.

Tyler had not seen his baby who now was three months old.

Sandy had no babysitter that day of the trial and had no money to pay for one, so she had taken the baby to court with her. This did not go over very well with the court officials, but she had no choice. While she was trying to defend herself, Tyler held his son and bonded with him.

He decided he wanted to be in his son's life. He had another motive money.

Sandy was depressed. She was passing the casino a week before the trial, and she decided to risk her last twenty dollars to see if she could save her house. She went to the dollar machines and sat down. She put the money in the machine and pushed the button. She lost. She did this again. She finally said a small prayer and used the arm at the side of the machine. Bells and chimes began ringing loudly. Sandy looked up and was stunned when she saw that she had won eleven thousand dollars. She used this money to pay her late mortgage payments.

The social workers were trying to convince her to let her home go and get into a geared to income home to help her financially. She knew in her heart that she was losing another home and her family would have to move again. She just was not ready to accept it yet. This win gave the social worker more time to find her a geared to income place big enough to house her family. The social worker could only find a place in a women's shelter in the next town that was big enough. Sandy prepared to move there.

Tyler learned that Sandy had won a lot of money and suddenly he was coming over to see her and talking marriage again. What he wanted was to get her money so he could pay off all his bills. He tried to talk her into moving into a place with him. She refused to give him any money or move in with him. This angered him. He did not seem to realize that she did not trust him because he had beaten her up and broken the promise to her so she could keep her home. If she did not go into the shelter, she would be on the street and her children could be taken from her and George's third threat would come to pass. She also felt that Tyler helped George.

Tyler helped her move against his wishes, but he caused her trouble. He would show up at the shelter demanding to see his son almost every day. Men where not allowed into the shelter, but Sandy let him in because she was afraid of him trying to get custody of Carl if she refused him. His father was wealthy, and he would give Tyler money to pay for a lawyer. She did not have the money to fight him in court. She only had a little left of her winnings which paid for the move, the storage unit for all her extra furniture, and car repairs.

She knew that he would be furious when he found out that when she went and got Carl's health card and his social insurance number. The lady that was serving her told her that if the father had abandoned her that she could use her last name. She did use her last name so all her children would have the same last name as herself.

The manager of the women's shelter was upset. Tyler's presence was upsetting the other women who were living at the shelter. She finally sent Sandy a letter telling her that she had to move out. So Sandy was back searching for a place to live again after only three weeks in the shelter. Sandy told Tyler that he had to start meeting her elsewhere. He did not like this. He wanted to force her into a position where she had no chose but to move in with him. She began taking Carl with her to meet Tyler at the coffee shop.    She did not realize that he was only after her money. She happened to ask him, "Can I get forty dollars for your son's diapers?"

"Where is all your money?" asked Tyler.

"I spent it on trying to keep a roof over my children's heads, moving, storage of furniture etc." This dashed his hope of paying off his debts.

Terry came over to their table and Tyler introduced him to Sandy.

The two men began talking about a drywall job for Tyler to do. He asked for Terry's phone number so he could call him with the day he could start the job. When Tyler went to put the number into his phone it was dead. He asked Sandy to put Terry's number into her phone. He told Terry that he had his schedule in his truck and would call him later that day. Terry left and Tyler told her that he was a drug dealer and to stay away from him. When they got in the car, Tyler borrowed her phone and called Terry and set up a time for him to do the drywalling job that Terry had offered him. Not long after this, Terry kept texting her to go out with him for a coffee. She keeps refusing because Tyler told her to stay away from this man. She had also had enough with men who were involved in drugs.

Sandy was going to drive one of the girls in the shelter for a court date in another city down country. The girl was paying Sandy for the gas to go there. Sandy did not know how Terry found out about it, but he sent her a message asking if she could pick up his girlfriend in that town and bring her back to this town to visit him. He offered her forty dollars. Sandy needed money to pay for her son's diapers.

When Tyler found out about Sandy doing this for Terry, he was livid. She tried to tell Tyler that she had not even see Terry. His girlfriend was the one who had given her the money. She told him that if he paid her child support for his son, she would not have to do things like this to make ends meet. This made Tyler even more angry. He felt like she betrayed him with this other man. He wanted revenge.

Three days later, Sandy came out to her car and found all the locks on her car had been busted. Tyler took her out for a coffee later that evening and again Terry showed up to talk to Tyler. When Tyler asked Terry back to Sandy's place, she was shocked. She tried to argue with him to change his mind because he knew that she had got the letter from the shelter manager. He bullied her into letting them come over. While she was busy getting the children to bed, Tyler and Terry went outside for a smoke. While they were out in the courtyard. One of the ladies in the shelter saw Tyler give Terry some drugs.

Terry left shortly after that. Tyler stayed and watched as Sandy bathed the baby in the kitchen sink. Carl splashed and giggled as he played with his mother as she wiped him all down with a washcloth.

She then took him out of the water and laid him on a towel to dry him off. She asked Tyler to get her a diaper out of her diaper bag. He did and he noticed that she only had a few diapers left.

"Where do you keep your extra diapers, and I will put some in your diaper bag?"

"That is all the diapers I have," Sandy said. "I have to get some at the store in the morning." early and start this new drywall job I got." Tyler went to the door followed by Sandy holding the baby. He went out turned and waved. The baby waved back as Sandy shut the door and locked it. She finished getting the baby ready for bed.

The next morning, Sandy got the older children ready for school and out the door. She then got herself and the baby ready to leave.

She was driving down the street when she saw Terry waving her down. As she neared him, he stepped out in front of her. She stopped or she would have hit him. He ran and jumped into the car beside her. He asked if she was going to the mall because he needed a ride there.

She nodded yes. She was shocked when he jumped into the car with her. Why? Was a ride all he wanted?

Her uneasiness increased when she stopped by the police car two blocks later.

"Why did you pull me over?" Sandy asked the policeman that came up to her window. "Do I have a signal light out?"

"No, I need you and your companion to get out of the car slowly and keep your hands in sight."

Sandy did not know what to think. She had not done anything wrong.

"Could you get your baby out of the car seat so we can search your car?"

"Why are you searching my car?"

"We had an informant call us telling us that a car of your colour, and your model with your license plate number would be carrying drugs."

"I don't use illegal drugs," said Sandy as she got the baby out of his car seat. The policewomen searched Sandy and the baby for drugs. She then got the diaper bag out of the back seat of the car and searched it while Terry had already been handcuffed. The policeman had pulled two bags of drugs out of the seat cushions on Terry's side of the car. The policewoman found one tiny, white pill loose in the bottom of the diaper bag. They then put Sandy into a cruiser and took her to the police station with the baby. She was crying the whole time telling the driver of the cruiser that she was not involved with illegal drugs in any way.

They put her into an interview room with the baby and proceeded to call CAS to get a social worker for the children. In the meantime, the two policemen came into the interview room and started to ask Sandy questions.

"Where were you going today?"

"I was going to the mall to get diapers for my baby," she said as she squeezed her baby and began to cry.

"Who knew that you were going there?"

"Tyler, the baby's father knew. He was the only person who knew."

"Why was Terry with you?"

"I was driving. I saw him on the sidewalk waving me down and when I got closer, he stepped out in front of me. I stopped before I hit him. He then ran to the car door and jumped into the car," Sandy said between sobs.

"Did you know him?"

"The father of my baby knows him and introduced him to me a few weeks ago." Sandy said, "He told me that Terry was a drug dealer so when he got in the car, I felt scared that he might do something to hurt me or my baby."

"Who is the father of your baby?" "Tyler Collins"

"We will be charging you."

Sandy did not know what to do. She knew she could go to jail for this, and she was scared because the police did not seem to want to believe her. She knew she would need a lawyer, but she didn't have money to pay for one.

Shortly after this, the CAS lady showed up and she demanded that Sandy have her hair tested to prove that she was not using so she could keep her children. Sandy asked to make a phone call to her family lawyer, he was an ex-boss of hers.

Her lawyer told her not to take the hair test because Sandy had told him that she was on Ritalin for her ADHD. He told her that even women who used hair products and over the counter drugs will test positive for illegal drugs because these products have a trace of these illegal drugs in them. They then lose their children and had to fight to get them back. He told her not to take the test because the Ritalin she was on is called methylphenidate which means the test would say she was using meth. He told her to stop using the Ritalin and wait at least a week before she takes any test.

When Sandy refused to take the test, the CAS lady started harping at her that she was going to take her children away from her as soon as they got home from school. This upset Sandy even more and she began saying over and over that she was not using anything but her prescription drugs She went on that she is a good mother who but the loved her children. She repeated this over and over as tears streamed down her face. She seemed to be in a form of shock. The CAS lady proceeded to call the school. She told them that Lynda was the one to call if she had an emergency. Lynda was called but no one would tell her what was going on. They just told her that they would have the children at the house waiting for her arrival.

The police station was across the street from the women's shelter so when Bob and Lynda were driving past the police station, they spotted Sandy's car parked in the parking lot with a man sitting in it.

Lynda wondered who this man was and why was he in her daughter's car.

When they pulled into the women's shelters parking lot the children ran out to them. They were scared. The teacher that had brought the children home left as soon as their grandparents showed up. No one told any of them what was happening. They went in and waited for Sandy or someone to tell them what was going on.

Not long after that Sandy walked in with tears running down her face and holding the baby tightly to her chest. The CAS lady followed behind her harping at Sandy to take the drug test.

Sandy kept telling her that her family lawyer had told her not to take the test because the Ritalin she was taking for her ADHD would come up as meth in a hair test. Her lawyer had told her about another test that they had which would tell the exact drug that the person had in her system. Sandy called her doctor to ask about this test. She told Sandy that she did not know what test that was. Sandy called the hospital and arranged to take the test that would tell them what was in her system. She was going to take a test every two days or three days.

Sandy sat down with her parents and told them everything that had happened. Lynda immediately thought that it was a setup. Bob, of course, thought that Lynda's idea was crazy. All the CAS lady, would say, was that she was going to take Sandy's. children away from Sandy because she was accused of drug trafficking and would not take the drug test. This upset Sandy who sat crying saying over and over that she was a good mother and she only used prescribed drugs or over the counter products. She repeatedly told the CAS lady that she was on Ritalin but the lady would not believe her.

The CAS lady let it slip that Sandy had a history of drugs to Lynda who knew this was untrue. She had known that George had accused her often of using drugs to the CAS and her co-workers. Tyler had already told all his family that Sandy was a drug user. His sister worked for CAS, so his sister had every reason to believe her brother. He had used that excuse to explain away the black eye she had given him. He had not told anyone that he had beaten Sandy up. Neither had she out of fear of Tyler. Did Tyler's sister who worked at CAS influence this lady into believing that that Sandy was a user? Sandy had proved to the court when George challenged her for the children that she was not a user two years before this.

The CAS lady kept insisting that she needed the test, or she would take the children immediately. Lynda happened to have the next three days off. The CAS lady finally decided that if Lynda stayed with Sandy, the children could stay there.

Bob left because he had to get up early in the morning to go to work so he gave a kiss and hug to everyone and left. As he went out the locked door to the shelter, he told Lynda to keep him posted.

The CAS lady went around the house inspecting Sandy's place.

She was not happy when she saw that the baby's crib was broken. Sandy told her that Tyler had not fixed it yet. Sandy tried to keep the baby safe by setting up the junior bed she had. She put it up to the corner of the room against the wall and a side guard on it. If the baby got out of bed, he had to go down to the foot of the bed to get out.

Sandy also had a foam pad under the bed which she pulled out when the baby was in it so that if the baby did fall out of it. He would land on the four-inch pad and would drop less than eight inches from the top of the bed to the pad. This did not satisfy this lady. She insisted that if they did not have a proper crib for the baby by the next day, she was taking the children. Lynda wondered what this lady would do if she went into the house of some person who was using Montessori methods of raising her child. The CAS lady was upset because the child could get out of bed in the middle of the night. He was old enough that he was sleeping through the night.

After the CAS lady left, the doorbell rang again and this time it was Terry's girlfriend who wanted to tell Sandy that Terry wanted to talk to her. Lynda had answered the door. Sandy was crying her eyes out in the living room. Lynda called out to Sandy telling her who was at the door. Sandy yelled back that she did not want to talk to Terry because he cost her custody of her children.

# CHAPTER 11

The effect without the Ritalin to help Sandy focus was apparent to those that knew her. She was more emotional, and her thought process jumped around when she tried to explain things. Everyone who knew Sandy realized that she needed the Ritalin, but Sandy refused to take any medication from that point on.

The CAS lady would not even take Lynda's observation that if Sandy were hooked on drugs like the CAS lady was claiming she was. She would have gone into withdrawal in the three days that Sandy was with Lynda. Also, the baby would not have been a big healthy boy if she had been hooked on drugs during her pregnancy. She would not have gained eighty pounds carrying the baby. The boy would have been addicted to the drugs at birth if she had been using the way George and Tyler made it appear in the lies, they told people about Sandy.

Sandy needed to have someone take her children for her when Lynda went back to work. Problem was they only had Sandy's brother and his wife who could take the three older children. Everyone worked. Lynda and Bob had his parents living with them. His mother's heart was not working properly so they could not leave the baby with her. The CAS lady left saying she would be back the next day to take the children unless we had someone to take them.

Lynda knew in her heart that this had been a setup by Tyler. He was fulfilling George's threats one by one and in the exact order that George had threatened to do it. It was just too neat. She remembered that Tyler had said to them the first time they met him that he knew important people who would help him,

The police called Sandy and asked her to come back in for questioning that afternoon. She went and left the children with Lynda. The policeman escorted her into an interview room and told her to have a seat. Sandy sat down where they told her to sit as she nervously twisted a tissue in her hand.

"Where were you going when we stopped you?" asked the policeman.

"To the store to get diapers for the baby. I am innocent. I don't do drugs." She pleaded as tears ran down her face.

"Who knew that you were going there?"

"Tyler, the baby's father. He was the only one who knew that I planned to go to the store. Did he do this to me to hurt me again or force me to move in with him?

"Why do you think this?"

"He is angry with me because I will not move in with him. His visits to the shelter caused trouble for me to stay there. I have been told by the shelter manager to find a new place to live. If I can not find a place my children and I will be homeless."

"Did you know Terry?"

"Tyler introduced me to Terry about two weeks ago. Tyler was doing a drywall job for him. Tyler told me he was a drug dealer, so I was to stay away from him. I was driving one of the girls at the shelter to court and she was paying for the gas. Terry heard that I was doing this, and he asked if I would pick up his girlfriend and bring her back here and he would pay me forty dollars. I did it because Tyler is not paying me child support and I needed formula for the baby."

"Why were they both at the shelter last night?" the policeman asked.

"Tyler asked Terry over to my place. I told him no they could not go to my place." Sandy said as she wiped her eyes and then blew her nose. "Tyler would not take no for an answer, and I am afraid of him."

"Why?"

"He beat me up when I was seven months pregnant."

"Do you have proof of this?" "You do."

"What do you mean we do?" questioned the policeman.

"You have my phone. There are pictures in my phone dated June 4th his birthday," Sandy took her front tooth out. "There is also this, he ripped this out of my mouth that night" as she held up one of her front teeth. She sat weeping uncontrollably as she told them what he had done to her between sobs.

"If he beat you up, he should be charged for assault."

"I can not. He will hurt my baby." She pleaded. "The CAS lady is going to give my baby to him." she blew her nose and reached for another tissue. "I do not have anyone who can take my baby," she sobbed. The CAS lady does not believe me when I told her I was on Ritalin. am innocent and I am going to lose my children. Just like George said would happen to me."

"What do you mean by that?"

"Well, my ex-husband, the father of my other three children, threatened to make me lose my job, make me lose my house, and finally make me lost my children. He tried to accomplish this but failed. Tyler is his friend, and he accomplished all three things leaving me without a job, without a home, and now without my children. Tyler and George have taken everything that I ever wanted away from me."

"That is for the court to decide. Excuse me and my partner for a few minutes." The policeman said as he nodded to his partner and pointed at the door.

The policemen went and found the pictures of her injuries from the beating. They also looked up the assault on her by George and the witnesses had told the police of the threats that he had made against her. She was telling them the truth. The witnesses all heard George threaten to make her lose everything. They decided to charge Tyler with assault.

They came back into the room and proceeded to tell her that they intended to tell CAS of his attack on her, and they would be the one charging Tyler for assault not her. She was finger-printed, and her photo taken and before she was released. One policeman said that he believed that she was innocent and that he would send a letter to the judge telling him that.

When she went to leave, she saw the crown attorney that was a friend of Tyler. She wondered why he was at the police station. When she exited the building, she saw three policemen hiding at the side of the women's shelter which was across the street from the police station. Terry was walking toward the parking lot of the women's shelter. The policeman she had talked to grabbed her and pulled her back into the station. The officer proceeded to tell her that she had to wait to go home. She demanded to know what was going on. He admitted that they were using her phone to catch Terry in a drug deal.

Sandy panicked and told the police that the children and her mother were in her place alone. She asked to call her mother and tell her to keep the children inside the shelter's walls. Lynda was livid when she heard this. She felt that the police put Sandy and her children in danger if Terry thought that Sandy had any part in this sting operation.

The police told Sandy that they would tell Terry that she was not involved in this take down, but Sandy did not feel so sure that she was not in danger by their actions.

Not long after that the CAS lady showed up and again started harping at Sandy to take the drug test. Sandy had already gone to the hospital to see about getting the test that would show exactly what she had been on. She arranged to take the blood test every two or three days so she could prove that she was not using any illegal drugs.

The CAS lady called Tyler and told him to come and get his son.

She left before he arrived which was a shame in Lynda's mind because she missed seeing the pure hatred that Tyler had for Sandy. He was livid when he learned that she had been with Terry. She sat crying her eyes out when Tyler left with Carl. He threatened her by saying that he would make sure she would never see her baby again.

Sandy was devastated because the other three children were to go to their uncle's place when they got home from school that night. George had got his wish. She had lost her children and she would have to fight to get them back. Sandy got hold of her family lawyer and he started the process to get her children back. Lynda prepared to go home feeling like the weight of the world was on her shoulders  because she felt that this was a setup by Tyler but how could she prove it. Sandy lost her three older children for two weeks. With the baby, she lost sole custody of Carl. She got the child every other weekend. Her mother had to be with Sandy whenever she had the child.

# CHAPTER 12

While this was going on, Sandy was also trying to find a place to live. She took Lynda to an apartment that had three bedrooms that she was interested in. They saw it and they figured out that she could afford it. Sandy was about to call the manager of the apartment  building when Sandy got a call from the social worker that they found a geared to income townhouse for her to move into.

The next week, Sandy had already moved into the new place when Lynda came with the baby. They were shocked when Sandy went to change his diaper. His bottom was covered in a bloody oozing sores the size of a saucer. They immediately went and got him medicine to heal the diaper rash. This was the first of many times they had to get medicine for the baby. He was coming with earaches, colds, weight loss, and high fevers. His father was neglecting him. Yet the courts and the CAS would not investigate him because his sister was a CAS worker. Her family doctor even refused to give her the baby's medical record so she could give it to her lawyer. Sandy was also having trouble getting her own health records from the doctor.

While they sat outside with the baby on a blanket with his bottom exposed to the air to help him heal, they talked about the situation.

Sandy told Lynda that she had learned that Tyler had lived in this housing unit with his ex-girlfriend. A lot of the people in the area knew him. This worried Lynda. She was sure that he would use these friendships against Sandy.

Sandy also told her that Tyler was best friends with the crown attorney. Tyler had told her that he had an affair with this man's wife when he was with his ex-girlfriend. Sandy told Lynda that this man was at the police station when she had been called in for questioning. This scared Lynda because a co-worker had told her that the crown attorney had made a statement to the press that he was going to use this case as an example in how they deal with drug traffickers. This solidified Lynda's belief that this was a setup.

"Sandy, remember when we bought the house for you," Lynda asked.

"Yes,"

"Did Tyler ever mention what had gone on then?"

"Tyler told me that he made about one hundred thousand dollars on that deal and his ex-girlfriend got nothing out of her share of the house. Was George using that to make Tyler hurt Sandy? Lynda sat wondering. She finally decided that George was smart, but he did not know the people that could help in this plan against Sandy. That was Tyler's contribution behind this setup. Sandy kept saying that Tyler loved her but in Lynda's mind the only one Tyler loved was himself. He was narcissistic.

She told Sandy that Tyler's sister worked for CAS, and he had already told his entire family that she was on drugs to explain away his black eye that she gave him the night he beat her up and ripped a tooth out of her head, Lynda realized that this was the reason that the CAS lady was so sure that Sandy had misused drugs. She had seen all the reports of drug use.

Lynda told the counselors that this was a setup because of George's threat of make her lose her job, make her lose her house, and make her lose her children. They did not believe Lynda because George had made the threat not Tyler. Lynda said yes but Tyler was the one who accomplished all these threats in order that George had said them.

Sandy had found out that the police had not tested the pill they found because they would have had to use the entire pill. They would have had no evidence against her to show the court. If they had tested it, they would have no evidence against her because if was an over- the-counter drug for weight loss. Did Tyler tell the crown attorney not to test it? He would have known what it was.

Terry and her charges were separated so Terry got off with an illegal stop. While her legal aid attorney did not try to defend her at all. Instead, he made a deal with the crown attorney and told Sandy that if she signed the judgement charging her with possession of .008 mg. of drugs, she would get two years probation. If she did not sign it, she would go to jail.

She needed to protect her children from one father who was hooked on drugs and another one who was mean and vindictive. She had no choice but to sign the paper and take probation.

She then had to face Tyler in court for the assault case the police had instigated. She suffered with PTSS every time she saw him. After several months of appearing in court they got to the trail part of our justice system. The lady judge looked at the pictures of Sandy's injuries but said the pictures were taken to close so they could not distinguish where the injuries were. Sandy told her that they were selfies and she had extended her arm as far as she could. Sandy told her what each picture was including the fingerprints on her neck. She even pulled the false tooth out to show where he had ripped the tooth out of her head. The judge finally said that both sides were assaulted in the fight because of Tyler's shiner. So, she settled it with a peace bond. Tyler walked away with no punishment for her beating. Sandy was losing faith in the justice system. The judge did not even consider that she was seven months pregnant at the time of the assault.

The family judge ruled that Tyler and Sandy would each get a week with the baby, and they would exchange the baby at the exchange center because of the peace bond. This took Lynda out of the middle of having to get the baby and return the baby to Tyler. She also did not have stay with Sandy when she had the baby. The stress that had been put on Lynda caused her to have high blood pressure which put a strain on her heart.

The children were teased at home and at school by neighbour children. It got so bad that Buddy had to change schools to stop being bullied. Buddy who had Asperger's had even had to defend himself on the playground. Three boys started pushing him around. He told them to stop and when they did not Buddy took them off their feet and put them on the ground with a karate moves, he had learned. He then told them in front of their mother that he would not be bullied. Sandy's children started to stay in their house away from the bullies and name callers.

Sandy did not even report that her car had been broken into and the ignition was jimmied with a screwdriver. She did not report it to the police because they keep telling her that they did not believe anything she told them because she had signed that drug charge document which mean she was guilty, yet she claimed she was not. She tried to explain to them why she had signed it to protect her children, but they would not accept that answer.

She was going to the hospital every two or three days to get tested for the court to prove that she was not using drugs. She had probation meetings to go to into two different towns. The family court decided that she could get the baby one week and then his father could have him the next week. This meant another hour trip one way to exchange the custody of the baby every Sunday. While she had to attend family court because she was still fighting for sole custody of her child. She was also going to court over the snow day and another day when she was too sick to drive to the court.

During all this she also had to drive the other three children who were returned to her mother after two weeks. She was spending all her time driving from all these meetings trying to prove her innocence. She was doing everything she could to get custardy of her son. No one believed her except the counselor for the drug addiction that she was not an addict.

She was also trying to get FRO to help her get money out of George to help her financial situation but like usual they did little to help her. They never tried to make him lose his driver's license or his tickets for construction. By this time, he owed her about fifty thousand dollars in back child support and other childcare costs.

What made things worse was that her family lawyer told her to take videos of the baby crying and clinging to her when the lady at the exchange center tried to take him to his father. Sandy had asked her eldest child Patricia to take the video with her phone. The lady at the exchange center grabbed the phone away from Patricia. This angered Sandy because the lady was not going to give the phone back to her.

Sandy grabbed the phone, and the lady then told them that neither of them could come on the property again. Sandy tried to explain that she was only doing what her lawyer had asked her to do. The lady would not listen to her explanation. Sandy now had to have either her mother, father, or a friend take or return the toddler.

Sandy would park at a nearby church walk with the person doing the exchange to the edge of their property. The person would go in and get the child. Once they were outside, Carl would run into his mother's arms and be carried to the car to make the hour drive to her home.

Sandy had made friends with one of the guys living in the subdivision. He was going through a bad divorce. He could not have any children of his own. He loved going over to her place and playing with the children and watching cartoons with them.

He acted like a big kid when they were around. He also helped Sandy with chores that she did not have time for because she had an appointment to get to.

Eric was trying to stay drug free; Sandy told him he could visit any time if he was drug free. He ended up moving in with her which helped them both financially and gave her someone that she trusted in the area.

Tyler had also arranged that Sandy got her son the weeks that she had to go to court. This meant she had to pay for babysitting or get Patricia to stay home to babysit her brother. Sandy did not like keeping Patricia from her classes. Sandy had Eric babysit Carl.

Eric's presence in Sandy's life made Tyler angrier. He still loved Sandy, but she had not lived up to his idea of what his wife should be. He was jealous of anyone who was with her. What made matters worse was the Carl loved playing with Eric and he would tell his father about the things that Eric did with him. Tyler became jealous of Eric who he felt was winning a place in his son's heart.

This went on for about four months with no changes in their situation until on the way to the exchange center Sandy had a flat tire. When she looked in her trunk, she found that the jack had been stolen. She called the center to tell them that she was stuck on the side of the road with a flat tire and no jack. They called Tyler. He told them that he would get his father to come with him because of the peace bond. Half and hour later he showed up alone. Sandy never reported that he broke the peace bond that day.

When Carl saw his father, he started crying and screaming.

Sandy could not get him to calm down. Eric was helping a friend, so she had asked Margaret, her friend, to go with her to get Carl. She had never seen the toddler that upset. Sandy did not know what to do to calm him. She wondered if Tyler had abused the child. She knew Tyler was capable of abuse. Her PTSS set in.

This was the first time she had seen him with his son since he took custody of him. This made her very wary, nervous, and afraid of him. She knew that the child was neglected in the fact that he was sick with colds and earaches when he was turned over to her. She would go and get him medication and get him feeling better before he had to go back to his father only to be returned sick again the next week. Yet her requests to CAS to investigate Tyler where ignored. Even her request for his medical information was declined by the doctor because she did not have main custody of the child because of her police charges.

She got so upset that she put Carl in his seat and climbed in the car and drove away as soon as the tire was changed. Of course, that was breaking the court order. She did not go far because her girlfriend convinced her to calm down and return him to his father. She called Tyler on his phone saying she was sorry and that she would bring the child to him. He told her not to bother that they would just exchange him like usual the following Sunday.

By Monday, the police where at her door charging her so she had more court visits to make. What made it worse was that as usual Tyler twisted the truth to his advantage. He never told the judge that she had called him, and he was the one who suggested that she keep the baby for the week. No one seemed to care how upset the child had been when he saw Tyler.

What made matters worse was that one early morning she was on the road driving to get to a parole meeting. When she turned on the main highway, the sun was just rising over the horizon, and it was right at the road level. The sun was so bright it blinded her. She had an operation to correct her eyesight years before.        This left her sensitive to bright light. She normally wore sunglasses but when she got in the car, she could not find them.

She was right in the middle of a construction zone, and she followed the pilons, but she missed a turn into another lane, and she ran into a pile of white gravel. She damaged her car and gave herself a small concussion. This meant that she had to get Lynda to drive her to her appointments and to the court dates until she got a used car.

# CHAPTER 13

I n the meantime, Sandy was being Sandy, by trying to help anyone she could in the area. She soon discovered that a lot of the people in the area drug problems, medical problems, and financial problems.

A teenage mother who lived near Sandy, was struggling to make ends meet. To help Sandy would give her the baby clothes that her son had grown out of. They also babysat for each other. Sandy also showed her how to make baby food for the baby which is a lot cheaper than buying baby jars of food.

Sandy took Mindy, a known addict under her wing. She just had a baby but because of her addiction, she could not keep her child.

Mindy asked Sandy to help her mother fix up her house so she could get custody of her grandchild. Sandy spent a few days at her house cleaning, moving drugs and dangerous cleaning products up out of a child's reach, installing cupboard latches and other safety features.

When Mindy's mother got custody of the child, Mindy felt that she owed Sandy. This meant that she could go over every day and see her son. She came over to Sandy's every morning to have coffee and talk. Sandy encouraged her to go back to school or get a job. Mindy helped her when ever she could to repay her for Sandy's act of kindness, but she just was not ready to give up drugs.

Of course, the police watching Sandy's house was anxious to prove that Sandy was giving Mindy drugs to transport to take to other people. They watched Mindy but she never had drugs on her when she saw Sandy.

Sandy started to have spells where her left side was so painful, she could hardly move. She was nauseated and in a lot of pain, but she had no doctor. Her doctor refused, to care for Sandy after she missed an appointment months before this. She had one of these painful attacks and had been too sick to make the forty-five- minute drive to the doctor's office.

Anxiety and worrying was causing her to have gallbladder attacks, but she did not have time to go to the hospital and sit for hours to get tested to see what was wrong with her. She was running to appointments, the court, and the exchange center almost every day.

Tyler knew that Sandy was not taking these medications because of the drug tests she was taking. This made her get emotional and upset very easily. He used that against her. He knew that she was buying things at flea markets and garage sales. She would fix these items up and sell them online for extra money.

Tyler approached Margaret and her son to see if they would set Sandy up for another assault charge. In payment, Tyler supplied them with drugs. Sandy had befriended Margaret when she moved into the housing development. They had helped each other out so when Sandy had a couch for sale and the lady needed one but did not have the money to pay Sandy right away. Sandy agreed to wait to get paid until Margaret received her next cheque.

One month went by, then two months passed. Sandy tried to talk to her, but she would not answer her phone calls or texts. She would not open her door to Sandy. Sandy was hurt. What had she done to make her friend turn against her?

In the meantime, Tyler made sure that Eric was arrested by the police and thrown into jail. He was out of the way leaving Sandy all alone. Tyler knew that Sandy got upset easily, that was what he was counting on.

One night, Sandy received a message from Margaret to ask her to meet with her and talk. When Sandy told her that she would come  over immediately. Then she got a message forget it, but Sandy wanted to learn what happened to their friendship. When she got there the front door was locked and the lady would not open the door. The TV and the lights were on.  Sandy kicked the door in frustration. The door swung open. This surprised Sandy who stepped inside and called the lady's name.

The lady was in the kitchen and her son, Kyle, told her to go upstairs. Sandy pleaded with her to talk to her. As Margaret passed  by her and went up the stairs not saying a word to her. Kyle grabbed Sandy and began fighting with her. He was a young man who was over six foot tall and strong. He grabbed Sandy and began slamming her head into the walls Sandy did not try to do any harm to him because in the assault against Tyler, the charges were dropped because she had given Tyler a black eye.

She just tried to push him away so she could get out of there.

They spun round and around as they struggled. Sandy felt sick at her stomach every time her head hit the wall. She knew she was really hurt. He pounded her head into the wall a few more times and then the boy threw her out the doorway with all his might. Her head hit the cement steps hard. She saw stars. She feared for her life. She scrambled to her feet and ran home to safety.

She did not realize that she had just received severe concussion. When she got home, she locked the door and rushed upstairs to check on her children to make sure they were safe.

Patricia was sleeping when her mother came into her bedroom. She woke up when her mother shook her and told her that they were moving back to the town where Sandy's grandmother lived. Her grandmother had died a few years before this. Patricia did not know what was going on. Her mother then stood up and left the room, so Patricia went back to sleep thinking that her mother was sleepwalking, or she had dreamed this.

Sandy went down into the basement to start a load of wash like she did every night. Suddenly she felt sick. She went to the laundry sink and threw up violently. She then blacked out and fell onto the cold cement floor in a heap.

# CHAPTER 14

The police told her that they had come to her door and knocked that night when she told them she had passed out, they did not believe her. They just thought that she was trying to avoid them.

The children assumed Sandy was sleeping in. Since she had a couple of head injuries Sandy slept a lot. When they found their lunches ready in the frig for them to take to school, Patricia told the other two children to get ready for school. They had no idea that their mother was so severely injured.

She was still unconscious on the cold cement floor when Mindy came in and called out for Sandy. She did not hear the usual response of "I will be right down," from the bedrooms upstairs. She thought that Sandy had to leave early for court that day and left.

Sandy finally woke up around two thirty that afternoon. She had been on the floor unconscious for about sixteen hours. She woke up with a splitting headache. Sandy got cleaned up and when to the hospital. The doctor told her that she had a sever concussion and needed medication and rest. He gave her a dose of the medication and a prescription to fill. Sandy went home to get her medical card for social services so she could get the medication.

Before she could do that, the police surrounded her and arrested her for assault.

Lynda was called by the police to come and get the children.

Lynda was not really informed of exactly what was going on. That night after she got the children into bed, and she was preparing to lie on the couch and call Bob who would know what she had to do to get Sandy out of jail.

No one would tell her what charges Sandy faced. Lynda had only been to court twice in her life, which was when she got a divorced from Sandy's real father and when Bob adopted Sandy. Lynda did not even know where the courthouse was.

There was a knock on the door and the man that was there introduced himself as a friend of Sandy's. His name was Ivan. He told Lynda what he knew about the arrest, and he wanted to help. Ivan told Lynda that Sandy would come into court the next day and she would be charged. She would need bail to get out. Lynda did not know how to get Sandy bail, but Ivan said he would help her through the process. Ivan drove her to the courthouse, the following morning and set up the bail for Sandy to get released from jail.

Sandy had been crying. She looked terrible and was shaking as she was told that she was being charged with assault again.

Lynda put up bail for Sandy and she was released. When they got her out of the courthouse, she announced that she had to be back there in an hour for the family court session. They rushed into town and got her a dress, shoes, and make-up to wear at the court session.

She told them while they ate that the police had taken her to jail in another town the night she was arrested. She had asked to see a doctor because she had a severe headache. They refused her. She cried and cried in pain for hours until she finally got desperate and told the guards that she would kill herself unless they took her to a doctor.

They sent her to the infirmary and the doctor found she had a severe concussion and gave her the medicine she needed to relieve the headache she was suffering with.

Lynda was not allowed into family court because it was a

closed session. Tyler pushed for Sandy to get less time with her son because of his charge against her. Ivan and Lynda were shocked when Sandy walked out of the courtroom and announced that she had just fired her family lawyer because he was not helping her get custody of her son.

Sandy did not tell her family lawyer that she had a severe concussion and was not able to make wise decisions at that point.

The court took the one week with Sandy and one week with Tyler away and allowed Sandy to see her son every other weekend from Friday at five p.m. to Sunday at five p.m. only. He even requested that Lynda or Bob had to be with her the whole time. Sandy got so upset she stood up in court and fired her family lawyer. This angered him because he was the best in the area, and he was embarrassed about being publicly fired. He spread the word among the lawyers not to work for Sandy.

Sandy went to her probation officer to explain that Lynda worked part-time usually weekends and Bob worked every Saturday. That restriction was dropped.

Sandy was able to get a legal aid lawyer, a lady this time to defend her on the assault charges. As the trail date approached, the lady asked for Sandy's health records because she had put a request in for them and she was having trouble getting them.

Sandy did not realize that the concussions had changed her. She was forgetful and more unorganized. Even her answers to people's questions were confusing.

When her lawyer could not get Sandy's health record, Lynda pushed Sandy to get her health record. Sandy called the doctor's office, and she was told she had to go to the records department. She was told she had to pay for it, and she requested that she get the record from the three hospitals that she has gone to. Lynda paid the fee and waited. They called Sandy five times in the following three months telling her that she could pick the records up. When she got there, the records were not there. Once she even got a call asking her if she still wanted them.

Sandy had told Lynda that when Sandy had been charged with having drugs. Her doctor believed she was guilty because Sandy had been using Ritalin and she had not been the one who prescribed it.

She needed her records to show that she had ADHD, PTSS, and several concussions. The boy's assault had made her condition worse. She had asked the police to charge the boy with assault and they refused to do it.

Lynda also told her to get Carl's health record. Sandy had repeatedly asked the doctor to document all the illness and earaches, etc. that Carl had had since Tyler had taken custody of the child. The doctor refused to give it to her. Sandy wanted it for CAS to show them that Carl was being neglected.

Finally, she got a call that the records were waiting for her at the registration desk for the doctor's office. Lynda went with Sandy. Sure enough, they got there and the lady at the desk got up and went to her file cabinet and came back saying there was no records there for Sandy.

This angered Lynda. She said in a stern voice, "Enough is enough. If we do not have those records by tomorrow, I will be having my lawyer and the police looking into the matter. You have no right to deny this lady her health records or that of her son."

The next day they went back and got the records on a flash drive which was locked shut by a password. Lynda had to call and again push to get the information to unlock it so they could print the records out for her lawyer and the judge. They showed that Sandy was not using illegal drugs. It also showed that George, Tyler, and the assault by the boy had given her concussions which was later determined to have caused her permanent brain damage.

She was also having trouble getting paperwork she needed for court from CAS. The CAS lady promised that she would have the paperwork for her the morning for court. Sandy and Lynda left early to get it before they had to be in court. When they got there the lady started asking her again about the Ritalin she had been using and refused to give her the paperwork. This angered Lynda who wrote a letter to the supervisor of the CAS lady telling how she had treated them and a list of things that she was supposed to have done and had not. They never saw this lady again on the case.

Two weeks after the assault, Sandy was taking Eric to a job in a nearby town. As she was returning home, she began to feel sick. She was ten blocks from home. She pulled over and sat for awhile until she felt better then continued driving. Three blocks from home she passed out at the wheel. Her car ran into the back of a utility truck owned by hydro. Then another car ran into the back of her.

The cars were totalled. When the police got there, Sandy was just starting to come around. Sandy asked to be taken to the hospital. The police believed that she blacked out from the use of drugs. They refused to take to be checked out. Instead, they left her sitting on the curb for four hours. She called her children and told them where she was. She sat shaking and feeling sick at her stomach until her three children showed up with a coat for her and food. They brought crackers and water because she told them that she felt sick. The children sat with her. Patricia went and got them all food at a nearby restaurant. They were scared and shaken when they saw the car. She could have been killed.

Sandy experienced severe headaches which were so bad that she would go to the hospital. Each time she drove herself because no one had told her that she should not be driving.

Months after the accident the emergency doctor learned that she was driving herself to the hospital and he cancelled Sandy's driver's license. This meant that

Lynda had to drive her two or three times a week to the courthouse and lawyer's appointments and court appearances and the hospital for tests.

Again, they were not allowed into the court room to hear the testimony of the boy and his mother on the day of the trail. They had to go by what her lawyer told them. The boy himself had a few scratches and a torn shirt only. The lawyer told Sandy that the stories they told on the stand was full of flaws and contradictions.

She told Sandy that they had said there was a footprint on the door yet the police officer who answered the call never mentioned a footprint on the door. They had testified that this six-foot tall strong teenage boy was picked up by Sandy who was five foot five inches and twenty-five years older and swung the boy around and around in the small living room.

The lawyer had made a lot of points that showed the problem with their stories to the judge. She was so confident with her defense that she did not give the judge, Sandy's health records.

When Sandy got on the stand, she told the judge that she had a concussion and suffered from ADHD and PTSS. The judge used that against her because he kept asking her over and over if she had gone there to fight. He would not believe Sandy when she told him that she had gone over there to find out what she had done to turn this lady against her. Lynda had thought that the crown attorney would be the one asking Sandy the questions when she got on the stand. It was the judge who kept harping at her that she went to see the lady because she was angry. The judge pushed and pushed Sandy with the same questions over and over until she got emotional and confused with her mental conditions.

When she told them, what happened that the boy had grabbed her and started banging her head into the door that was leaning against the wall of the entrance hall. Her story was confused and emotional repeatedly saying that she did not know why the lady was angry with her. She told them that the boy threw her out of the doorway. She landed head-first on the cement steps. She feared for her life as she scrambled to her feet and ran home.

Her defense lawyer was shocked when the judge ignored her argument and found Sandy guilty. He gave her another two years of probation.

To make things worse the driver who drove into her tried to sue her for one million dollars. Of course, this led to more paperwork, meetings with her insurance company, and need for her medical information so she could win her case against the man. Sandy hoped that her insurance company would prove that she not using drugs. The police put the accident down to driving under the influence. The insurance company just followed the police report.

Three days later, at two o'clock in the morning, the police broke into her house with a warrant to search for drugs. They tore the house apart finding the paraphernalia for drug use and drugs in the house.

Eric had seen one cop taking a pipe and two small bags of white powder out of his pocket and pretending that he had just found them under the mattress in Sandy's bedroom. Eric immediately said that they were his to protect Sandy.

Other policeman started pulling things out of their pockets and pretending to find them in drawers under cushions.

"Great we finally got you," one policeman said to Sandy. While the woman policewomen moved in front of Sandy and backed her into a corner. She then stood in from of her like she was guarding her from her fellow policeman. The policeman that was guarding Eric did the same thing. This scared Sandy.

Again, Eric and Sandy were arrested. The children were taken to the police station. Lynda was called to come and get the children. It was three o'clock in the morning when Lynda got to the police station. At least this time she was told what the charges were. She was also told that no one was allowed in Sandy's house. She got the children from the police station and took them to her house. Lynda got the children off to bed. They were scared and confused at what would happen to their mother and them. If their mother went to jail, the children would have to go back to their father who they had not seen in a year or go into foster care and maybe split up. Lynda and Bob were both in their late sixties and were still working to make ends meet.

They could not support three pre-teenagers and a young boy.

Lynda got the children up the next morning. They decided that they wanted to go to school. Bob drove the children to their respected schools. When they got to the courthouse, Sandy was locked up in a waiting cell. She was brought into the courtroom. She was charged with possession of drugs. The trail date was set for over a year later.

The judge was going to put her into jail until one attorney asked why this lady who had not even had a parking ticket had gone on this spree of breaking the law.

He approached Bob and Lynda and asked if Sandy could be under house arrest at their home. She would only be able to go off the property if she were with one of them or was going to or from a meeting with her lawyer, court, or the parole office.

Bob and Lynda agreed since they now had no one living with them since Bob's mother had died and his father had had a major heart attack and was living in a nursing home. This would keep the grandchildren and their mother safe.

As Sandy walked by this one policeman, she said, "Nice to meet you but I hope I never see you again."

"Why did you say that to the policeman?" asked Lynda.

"He was one of the policemen who told me that there was a van outside waiting to take me to jail for the next few years." When I heard that I started to cry.

Bob drove to each school and picked up the children. Lynda and Sandy went into each school and started the process to change schools. Bob took the children to their new home. While Sandy and Lynda went to start the packing process at Sandy's place.

When they got there, the door was unlocked. The police had told them that her house was locked up and no one had been in it. Lynda was shocked when she went through the door. Three boys were sitting on the couch watching television.

Everything was torn apart, there was evidence that they had been doing drugs on the coffee table. One of the boys was Tom. Sandy flew off the handle at him because she realized that he was the one who had brought some of the drugs and paraphernalia into the house that the police found. Eric took the blame for it to protect her. She told them to get out and stay out.

The boys left before Sandy found her opened purse tossed on the floor with clothes piled up over it. When she looked inside, she found all her money was gone. She knew then where Tom had got the money for this party he had in her house. She was furious. Sandy called the police and told him who she found in the house and what they were doing.

Sandy and Lynda worked at packing a lot of boxes until seven o'clock that night. They loaded the car with clothes for everyone to the bursting point. They were just about to leave when the phone rang. It was the arresting police officer calling to tell Sandy that she had another charge against her for a stolen compressor. Lynda immediately got suspicious that this was another setup.

Mindy had stopped by all upset because Sandy would be moving away. When she heard about the compressor, she told Lynda that she had given that compressor to Sandy the day before she had been arrested. Mindy had found it in the dumpster behind the mall near their house. She gave it to Sandy because she liked to paint. Mindy called the police officer and told him that she was the one who brought it into

Sandy's house and that she had found it in the dumpster. Lynda had told the court at the last family court session that George had been  fired because Tyler had taken the owners compressor from the job site.

Sandy asked Mindy to stay the night at the house and make sure that Tom did not get back in. She told the police that Mindy would be spending the night in the house to keep them out.

When they went to drive Sandy's car, they found that the ignition was tampered with. Sandy had to used a screwdriver to start the car. They also discovered that the car did not have enough gas to get the car across the road to the gas station. One month later Sandy got a ticket for speeding on the express lane three hours away from there. Who had taken her car and what had they done with it.

They were exhausted when they walked into the Lynda's housel.

The kids had claimed their bedrooms and were watching TV when they walked in. Bob had got them pizza, so they were happy and content, but they knew that the threat of their mother going to jail was hanging over their heads and would be until justice occurred.

# CHAPTER 15

The next morning, the children wanted to come with them the house so they could say goodbye to their friends. They scattered to the wind when we pulled up to the Sandy's house.

When they entered the house, Mindy told Sandy that two boys tried to crawl in through the air conditioner hole and scared her half to death in the middle of the night. She had slept on the couch that night right near where they tried to get in. Mindy scared them away, but she did not want to sleep there again.

Sandy was upset by this because they could take things from the house and sell it. She called a friend of hers named Al and asked him if he would help her pack and stay at the house and keep people out of it. He agreed so on their next trip to the house, they picked him up and brought him there. He did a good job of packing. This gave Sandy and Lynda the time to get the children into their new school and on the bus route. They also informed everyone the change of address for Sandy.

By the weekend with Bob getting the use of his boss's delivery truck they got Sandy moved and her furniture in a storage unit. They cleaned up the place and she turned in the keys.

Less than two weeks later, Tyler's sister and her husband bought the house that was kitty-corner to Lynda's house. This really made Lynda suspicious of Tyler because they could see the side door of the house which was the door that everyone used to come in and out of Bob's place.

Sandy got to the point that when she wanted to have a

cigarette, she would go and sit in the garage with the door part way down so they could not see her smoking cigarettes. She was afraid that they would accuse her of smoking weed. The house was being watched Tyler's brother-in-law had set up a camera over their garage door which faced Bob's house.

On Halloween, Sandy took Carl out to trick or treat. The other children who were older went with their friends. Everyone but Lynda dressed up. When they got to Carl's aunt's place and the door opened, Carl saw his cousin and his brother. The child stepped back and looked at Lynda with wide eyed fear. His mother did not see this because she was at the door getting Carl's treats.

Then when the children started to ride the school bus.
Buddy rode it once. He would not go on it again. Instead, he walked to school three miles through every type of weather. He never told anyone why he wanted to walk to school.

Patricia started to miss classes and she was not doing well in school. Patricia announced that she was going with her boyfriend to tour the States with his band. She was going to be eighteen on her next birthday. Patricia was trying drugs and skipping school. She was doing everything to defy her mother. CAS got involved which made things worse.

Tammy spent all her time in her bedroom except to come out to eat. He also loved to upset Patricia. This lead to Sandy having to step in and break them up.

The only good thing that occurred was a biker approached Sandy.

She was told that the police of the town she had moved from was under investigation shortly after she moves to her parent's house. They were being investigated by the RCMP. Sandy did not know what to believe until the next Monday morning. She had to go to the police station every Monday before 11 o'clock to sign in. If she did not do this, they would put out a bulletin to pick Sandy up. That morning Sandy was running late so they got there a few minutes after 11 o'clock. Two RCMP officers stood there talking about the accident the night before that killed two teenagers.

Lynda hoped that Sandy would be forgiven for bring late. Sandy went to the list and signed her name. She then turned to Lynda and said, "Let's go."

"Excuse me, ladies. Could we ask you a few questions?" as he ushered them into a large room. A table and four chairs were there with a recorder set up on it. Lynda and Sandy were a little shaken by this, but it gave Lynda a chance to show people that Sandy was innocent.

There have been a few questions that have come up about your charges. Please answer our questions truthfully and fully."

"What do you want to know?" asked Lynda.

"I am innocent," moaned Sandy. "The drug they found in my diaper bag was an over -the-counter weight loss pill to help me get rid of the eighty pounds I have gained caring my baby. The pill is not illegal. If they had tested it, they would have used it all and would have no evidence against me. ", said:

"These are the reasons everyone thinks that she is guilty," Lynda

".1 George broke into Sandy's house and found her medication.

It was Ritalin otherwise known as Methylphenidate at the time. He did not know that she was diagnosed with ADHD and PTSS. He assumed she was using. He used this information to try to make her lose her job which was his first threat."

"2. George used that information to make CAS believe that she was a meth user. His mother and him called them repeatedly causing CAS to investigate Sandy but they never found drugs."

"3. Sandy got blood poisoning from an abscessed tooth and lost a lot of weight. She ended up having to have anti-biotics intravenously for a week.'

"4. Tyler told his family that Sandy was using drugs the night that she gave him the shiner. He used this to cover up the fact he had beat her up when she was seven months pregnant."

"5. Tyler's sister works for CAS so she could have seen all the reports that George had made, and she could have told the lady who was the one that came here that day. That lady would not believe one word we told her. Months later she called me up and asked if it was true that Sandy was on Ritalin. The day that Sandy was charged she stopped all her medication, and she has not been on it since so her blood tests at the hospital shows she is drug free to get the custody of her child back. The other children she got back in two weeks and custody of her baby. Her lawyer has her printed health records which shows she was not using. "

"7. The day of the trial, her lawyer made a deal with the crown attorney. If she said she was guilty she would get two years of probation. If she did not sign the paper saying she was guilty she would go to jail for two years. She was the sole guardian for these children. Older children have a father who was a drug addict and was considered an unfit father. They would most likely get split up by the foster care system. The baby would go to a father who tried to kill him when he beat Sandy up. He had custody right now and every time we get the baby, we must get medicine for him because he has infected ears, colds, etc.," said Lynda."

"I am innocent." Sandy said as she blew her nose.

"Is this all true?"

"George made the threats that he was going to make me lose my job, lose my house, and lose my children. He tried but I got a new job, got a new house, and only lose my three children for two weeks."

"W hat about when the police raided your house?" asked the older policeman.

"They came in and started tearing the place apart. One officer pulled a drawer open and then pulled out a small bag of white powder from his pocket. He turned to me and said, "We finally got you?"

"Eric immediately told them it was his. He was protecting me and the children. Others started pulling things out of their pockets and placing it under pillows. Then taking pictures of where they had put it," said Sandy. "One thing was strange. When the first officer put the drugs in the drawer and made the comment, the lady officer backed me into a corner and stood there like she was guarding me from her companions. The officer that was guarding Eric did the same thing."

"You have given us some things to think about," said the older policeman.

"I hope so," said Lynda as she followed Sandy out to the car.

# CHAPTER 16

The next time they were scheduled to go to the courthouse, Sandy's lawyer called her and told her that we did not need to go. The charges against her had been dropped. This was great for Sandy and Lynda.

It was not good for Eric. He had already lost his place to stay when the man who gave him shelter and put up his bail, passed away with cancer. Eric began taking drugs again. Sandy was helping him seek into Bob's house late at night in the winter months against Bob's wishes.

One month later the last of her probations were done. She decided it was time to go back out on her own. She found an apartment that she could afford. She was not there long before.

Patricia was skipping classes, falling asleep in classes, and doing drugs to keep awake. This upset Sandy and CAS. They stepped in and told Patricia that she would be taking summer classes. She wanted to go with her boyfriend on tour in the States with his band. She was not eighteen yet, which caused trouble with the CAS lady. She insisted that she go to summer school. Patrica called her father and asked if she could go live with him. Less than a year later she was in her own apartment and her boyfriend stayed with her when he was in town with his band. The next summer the two of them went on the tour. Patricia stopped talking with her mother.

Tyler showed up with paperwork saying that she could no longer see her son, but George would take her children to see him every month. Sandy was shattered. She had no money to fight him in court. For the truth to come out that she was never on illegal drugs. George and Tyler were the ones who had done everything they could to hurt her.

They twisted a truth into a lie. Sandy wonders if the truth will ever come out and she will be able to unite her family again.